SMOOTHIE COOKBOOK

Cleanse Your Body and Boost Your Immune System With Delicious Smoothies

(How to Make a Perfect Smoothie Recipes)

Lionel Allen

Published by Sharon Lohan

© **Lionel Allen**

All Rights Reserved

Smoothie Cookbook: Cleanse Your Body and Boost Your Immune System With Delicious Smoothies (How to Make a Perfect Smoothie Recipes)

ISBN 978-1-990334-44-3

All rights reserved. No part of this guide may be reproduced in any form without permission in writing from the publisher except in the case of brief quotations embodied in critical articles or reviews.

Legal & Disclaimer

The information contained in this book is not designed to replace or take the place of any form of medicine or professional medical advice. The information in this book has been provided for educational and entertainment purposes only.

The information contained in this book has been compiled from sources deemed reliable, and it is accurate to the best of the Author's knowledge; however, the Author cannot guarantee its accuracy and validity and cannot be held liable for any errors or omissions. Changes are periodically made to this book. You must consult your doctor or get professional medical advice before using any of the suggested remedies, techniques, or information in this book.

Table of contents

Part 1 1

Introduction 2

Chapter 1: What Exactly Is A 12-Day Green Smoothie Cleanses? 5

Most Common Health Improvements After The 12 Day Green Smoothie Cleanse: 7

1.1 Why Do You Need A Cleanse, Green Or Otherwise? 9

Chapter 2: How To Do The 12-Day Green Smoothie Cleanse 12

Full Cleanse: 13

DRINK SMOOTHIES: 13

EAT SNACKS: 14

Beverage WATER AND DETOX TEA: 14

KEEP BOWELS MOVING? 14

Drink Smoothies And Eat One Healthy Meal: 14

EAT SNACKS: 15

Beverage WATER AND DETOX TEA: 15

KEEP BOWELS MOVING: 15

Chapter 3: The Shopping List 16

3.1 Food For The First Six Days 16

3.2 Food For The Last Six Days 17

Chapter 4: Benefits Of A Smoothie Lifestyle 18

Easy To Make And Are Portable 18

Alkalizing & Detoxing 19

Anti-Inflammatory 19

They Help Prevent Kidney Stones 19

They Fill You Up 20

Natural Weight Loss 20

Clearer Skin 21

Mental Clarity And Focus 21

Cancer Prevention Agents 21

Expanded Energy 22

They Make You Sexy 22

4.1 What Are The Best Greens For Your Smoothie? 22

Milder-Tasting Greens: 25

Stronger-Tasting Greens: 25

Chapter 5: What To Include In Your Green Smoothie 27

Chapter 6: Post Cleanse 29

Sample Meal Plan: 30

Chapter 7: Additional Information 32

Recipes: 33

Berry Peachy 33

Pineapple Spinach 34

Peach Berry Spinach 35

Pineapple Berry 36

Day 9: Apple Mango 37

Pineapple Kale 38

Conclusion 39

Part 2 41

Introduction 42

Chapter 1: Home Prepared Smoothies 44

Chapter 2: Benefits Of Healthy Smoothie Recipes 48

Chapter 3: Low Calorie Smoothies To Help You Lose Weight
.... 50

Chapter 4: How To Make A Healthy Drink With The Smoothie
.... 53

Chapter 5: Green Smoothie Recipes 55

1. Mint Mojito Green Smoothie 57

2. Love Your Body Green Smoothie 59

3. Avocado Grapefruit Green Smoothie 61

4. Kale Aide Green Smoothie 62

5. Apple Kale Green Smoothie 64

6. Restorative Detox Green Smoothie 65

7. Holiday Detox Smoothie 66

Chapter 6: Easy And Tasty Smoothie Recipes For Healthy Living 67

1. Peanut Butter And Jelly Protein Smoothie 70

2. Spinach Flax Protein Smoothie 71

3. Skinny Oreo Milkshake 72

4. Sunrise Smoothie 73

5. Dark Chocolate Peppermint Protein Shake 74

6. Almond Butter Chia Smoothie 75

7. Healthy Coffee Banana Smoothie Ingredients: 76

8. Grape And Blueberry Protein Smoothie 77

9. Berry Oat Breakfast Smoothie 78

10. Chocolate Peanut Butter Banana Breakfast Shake 79

11. Blueberry Almond Butter Smoothie 80

12. Raw Chocolate Smoothie 81

13. Raw Banana Bread Shake 82

14. Peach & Oat Breakfast Smoothie 84

15. Carrot Cake Smoothies 85

16. Apple Almond Flax Smoothie 87

17. Avocado + Lime Green Tea Smoothie 88

18. Strawberry Beet Smoothie 90

19. Grapefruit Green Smoothie 91

20. Clementine Sunshine Smoothie 92

21. Key Lime Pie Breakfast Smoothie 94

22. Matcha Mint Chip Smoothie 96

23. Healthy Peanut Butter Cup Smoothie 97

24. Kale-Ginger Detox Smoothie 99

25. Blueberry Coconut Lime Smoothie 100

26. Green Apple Pie Smoothie 102

27. Kiwi Basil Smoothie 104

28. Vanilla Date Smoothie 105

29. Superfood Power Smoothie 106

30. Raspberry Cheesecake Smoothie 109

31. Chocolate Covered Cherry Protein Smoothie 110

32. Chai Gingerbread Smoothie 111

33. Cinnamon Roll Smoothie 113

34. Apple Cinnamon Blueberry Smoothie 114

35. Eggnog Smoothie 116

Kombucha and Spinach Smoothie 118

Cayenne and Arugula Smoothie 119

Spicy Hot Smoothie 121

Flax Seed and Kale Smoothie 123

Cacao and Avocado Smoothie 124

Watermelon and Turmeric Smoothie 126

Dandelion and Banana Smoothie 127

Green Tea and Spinach Smoothie 129

Strawberry Arugula Smoothie 130

Kale and Lime Smoothie 131

Mango and Avocado Smoothie 132

Dandelion Greens and Mixed Berry Smoothie 133

Baby Spinach and Pear Smoothie 134

Spicy Spinach Smoothie 135

Romaine Lettuce and Ginger Smoothie 136

Radish and Greens Smoothie 137

Chard and Banana Smoothie 139

Kiwi Celery Smoothie 140

Spinach and Mixed Berry Smoothie 141

Banana, Spinach and Pineapple Smoothie 142

Chard and Coconut Smoothie 143

High Protein Pear Smoothie 144

Orange Smoothie with Spinach 145

Orange Protein Smoothie with Kale 146

Green Smoothie with Orange and Ginger 147

Green Smoothie with Mint and Blueberries 148

Green Smoothie with Kale and Pineapple 149

Rolled Oats Breakfast Smoothie 150

Honeydew Smoothie with Lime 151

Peaches and Kale Smoothie 152

Pineapple Avocado Smoothie 153

Agave, Spinach and Kale Smoothie 154

Spicy Green Smoothie 155

Honey and Spinach Smoothie 156

Apple and Greens Smoothie 157

Avocado and Lime Smoothie 158

Basil and Chlorella Smoothie 159

Berries and Beets Smoothie.. 161

Dandelion Smoothie with Lime... 162

Avocado and Mango Smoothie 163

Guacamole Smoothie... 164

Spinach and Strawberry Smoothie... 166

Cinnamon and Spinach Smoothie 168

Wheatgrass and Goji Berry Smoothie.. 169

Aloe Vera and Blueberry Smoothie.. 171

Strawberry Smoothie with Mint.. 172

Banana and Rosemary Smoothie.. 174

Beet Greens and Cinnamon Smoothie... 175

Spinach and Mint Smoothie 176

Kale Smoothie with Blueberries 177

Banana and Beets Smoothie 178

Mixed Berry and Lettuce Smoothie.. 179

Greens on Greens Smoothie... 180

Apples, Apples, Apples Green Smoothie 181

Banana and Mint Smoothie.. 182

Strawberry and Salad Smoothie 183

Banana and Romaine Lettuce Smoothie**Error! Bookmark not defined.**

Kiwi and Spinach Smoothie .... **Error! Bookmark not defined.**

Kale and Green Apple Smoothie**Error! Bookmark not defined.**

Kombucha, Cinnamon and Kale Smoothie**Error! Bookmark not defined.**

Conclusion 185

Part 1

INTRODUCTION

Every day all we hear and see is how slim, physically fit individuals are way more attractive. This has caused hype or each one of us to constantly searching for ways to lose weight as quickly as possible. Recently juice and smoothie cleanse and detox is becoming popular. Smoothie cleanse does not only cater to weight loss but also energizes you more by throwing out the toxins out of the body.

Battling with obesity and weight problems can be the most draining, challenging, frustrating experience. For some people, weight reduction is a constant struggle. Despite the fact that there are a lot of diets, pills and exercises available, the weight problem is rising day by day. Diet industry is huge and is earning lots of money by confusing people. The majority of the people who follow these diet plans to quickly lose weight fail to realize that this way they will rapidly gain back the weight. What each f we need to realize is that in order to get permanent weight loss you will have to make some lifestyle changes.

So what does it mean by a lifestyle change? Usually, people go on a diet which means that eventually at some point they will have to stop being "on the diet". In a typical scenario, once you go off the diet, you gain all the weight back on. So with this 12-day green smoothie cleanse what is encourage is for you to train your taste buds to eat and drink healthier foods. This way you will never have to think about dieting again.

The first step towards weight reduction is detoxification. Without detoxification, a huge number of individuals overall lose the battle to get thinner permanently. There are numerous elements that add to weight gain, and one element that is most neglected by customary weight control plans is toxic overburden.

Basically, individuals regularly experience issues shedding pounds on the grounds that their bodies are loaded with toxic substances. The more poisons you take in or are presented to consistently, the more poisons you store in fat cells in the body. Toxins that are stored in fat cells are hard to dispose of through eating fewer carbs alone. You should first detoxify the body. Along these lines, the most powerful health improvement plans ought to concentrate on both fat loss and detoxification, which prompt generally enhanced wellbeing and health.

Juice smoothies are marked as ideal courses on how you can clean your body from the destructive poisons that cause genuine ailments. You likewise have the alternative of including a portion of the best detox supplement keeping in mind the end goal to get the best result. A good thing about the juice smoothie is that it is fit for giving your body the required minerals, for example, fibres. On the off chance that you compare the smoothie cleanse from the juice cleanse, you will see that the strands are not separated in a smoothie shape simply like whole veggies or fruits that are mixed together.

As should be obvious, fibres are greatly vital for you as it is the responsible in uprooting the poisons inside your body. The juice cleanse is thought of as a light method for body detoxing as your digestive track still works normally as a result of the consumption of the fibre. The smoothie is likewise fit for fulfilling your craving and will help your digestion system in the meantime because of the fibres it will give to your body.

Uplifting news for everybody, custom made smoothies are not hard to make. All you will need is to set up the required ingredients and materials on your side, for example, blender and differed sorts of fruits. Figuring out how to make your own particular smoothie is simple, opposite to what you used to think. As long as you follow the right directions, you will get the perfect smoothie. By simply taking after the directions legitimately, you will get the outcomes you are searching for.

The 12 day Green Smoothie Cleanse is an amazing way to communicate to your body that you are going to do things differently from now on. Your purpose could be to purify your body or remove mucus so that you can heal better, reduce weight and get healthy. Or maybe you just want to eat healthily.

CHAPTER 1: WHAT EXACTLY IS A 12-DAY GREEN SMOOTHIE CLEANSES?

Detox/ cleanse is a stylish word in beauty and health circles. It is short for detoxification, which alludes to expelling poisons from your body or purifying your body of chemicals and pollutants. Detoxing is a fundamental part of keeping up and accomplishing lively wellbeing, and can likewise be a quick course to getting more fit.

Every day we are bombarded by chemicals and poisons every day. These originate from the foods you eat, the air you inhale, the beauty items you apply to your body, and numerous different things you come into contact with. Preferably, we'd abstain from coming into contact with all the bad agents, however, that is unrealistic. So the best way to go about is to eat healthy so that you can get the toxins out.

A better way to deal with restricting and getting rid of toxins from your body is to utilize normal and small detox methodologies. This may incorporate exercising each day, taking a sauna, drinking a lot of pure water, rehearsing dry skin brushing, and eating natural foods. You can likewise detoxify your body a little by creating smoothies that have natural detoxifying ingredients. There are numerous ingredients that are delicious, nutritious, and promote toxic discharge that function admirably in smoothies. Incorporate these in your smoothies to keep your body perfect and healthy.

On the off chance that you are searching for the compelling way on the best way to shake off your bad eating habits/ patterns or to keep up a healthy body, something you can do is to do the smoothie cleansing. Besides, before you get excessively excited about it, the first thing you have to do is to decide how your body will respond on having a negligible measure of protein or calories for every day. This is because it is critical that your body is getting the correct food as you attempt to take out the waste and liquids.

The 12-Day Green Smoothie Cleanse is a detox program that will offer you some assistance with losing weight, increment vitality, decrease cravings, and enhance general wellbeing. You will detoxify your body through an elimination of specific nourishments for twelve days and reinvent your taste buds to seek sound, supplement-rich foods. After you complete the smoothie cleanse, you will never need to count the number of calories you intake or take after confusing or costly diet plans or measure nourishment again. Your body will automatically pine for and wish healthy, natural foods.

Amid the 12-Day Green Smoothie Cleanse, you will give your body the quality nourishment it needs while purifying your cells and internal parts. Vitamins, minerals, and different supplements will be consumed by your body all the more effectively, permitting your cells to end up like new as you look and feel more youthful. What makes us feel old is slime and waste in the body. Cosmetic surgery and anti-aging creams aren't magical enough to clean that out.

Your skin will look younger in light of the fact that your cells will get to be tighter and also healthy. Maturing, dull, dry skin; puffiness; dark circles; and wrinkles will begin to blur away. It is conceivable to look and feel better. You will feel like you're becoming more youthful, not older than you are! To put it plainly, you'll figure out how to wind up youthful, sound, and lively from the inside out.

The 12-day green smoothie cleanse is the method of detox/cleanse made up of green leafy veggies, water and fruits. These green Smoothies are filling, healthy and you will like drinking them. Your body will likewise thank you for drinking them. You can hope to lose some weight, expand your vitality levels, decreased cravings, clear your mind, and enhance your absorption/digestion and your health. It is an ordeal that could change your life in the event that you stay with it!

Most Common Health Improvements After The 12 Day Green Smoothie Cleanse:

- Weight Loss (Most lose 10-15 pounds on the off chance that they adhere to the regimen)
- Increased vitality
- Mental clarity
- Better rest
- Decrease in cravings
- Less bloating and better digestion

The 12-day cleanse is a genuinely life-changing and health transforming experience. Here are the essential rules:

1. You will drink up to 72 ounces of green smoothies every day. Basically prepare your whole days of green smoothies in the morning and pack it up to take it with you. Keep it refrigerated however much as could reasonably be possible. Drink ¼ at one time every 3-4 hours for the duration of the day.

2. You may snack on celery, apples, carrots, cucumbers, and other crunchy vegetables that appeal you for the duration of the day. Other high-protein snacks incorporate unsweetened peanut butter, hard boiled eggs and unsalted nuts and seeds (just a handful).

3. Drink no less than 8 glasses of water (64 ounces) every day and herbal teas, as coveted.

4. Try not to EAT: white sugar, meat, dairy, alcohol, beer, espresso, soft drinks/diet soft drinks, prepared carbs (white bread, pasta, doughnuts, and so forth.)

The 12-day green smoothie challenge requires you replace breakfast and lunch with delicious clean drinks (2-3 of them) for 12 days. This has to be a drink that boosts energy. In addition to this, ou also has to drink 8 glasses of water every day. For your snacks, you can opt for raw almonds, apples or bananas. For dinner, you will have a light meal that is made up of greens.

Experiment this strategy for a week and then continue to see results. The third vital step for this program is to exercise. You need to find a physical activity that you enjoy and then work out for minimum half an hour each day. Whether it is Yoga, running, cycling or jogging. After 12 days, your body will be addicted to this lifestyle and you will incorporate healthy habits in your life.

1.1 WHY DO YOU NEED A CLEANSE, GREEN OR OTHERWISE?

Green or not green, smoothies have the great effect on your body. Today, we live in the world where we are constantly surrounded by pollutants. The air we breathe is not pure anymore, and this is why we absorb a lot of toxins from the environment. These toxins then make as lethargic and makes it difficult for us to lose weight. There are two types of toxins; environmental and metabolic toxins. Metabolic toxins are also known as endogenous toxins and are produced by each of our cells as they carry out their daily metabolic procedures.

Metabolic poisons can likewise be delivered by microorganisms that follow up on not entirely processed nourishment in your digestive tract. It's typical for your cells to contain a few poisons at all times. All things considered, your cells need to make vitality on a progressing basis, and the assembling procedure results in waste (poison) production. Poisons just present a test to your wellbeing when they accumulate.

The great news is that your body is intended to continually get together and expel poisons from your cells. The majority of the toxins that are mixed up from your cells are separated in your liver and afterward eliminated from your body by means of your kidneys, colon, skin, lungs, and bodily fluid linings in your nose and ears.

Put another way, every time that you urinate, poop, and breathe out, exhale, sniffle, and experience an inside-out reaction with your skin, your body kills poisons from your framework.

In the event that your levels of toxins in the body rise, your body expands its output through the eliminative channels. In the event that your eliminative components can't stay aware of the number of poisons that are coming in and being created in your cells, with an end goal to safeguard your health, your body stores the toxins in the fat tissues. All that really matters is this: Your body is focused on dispensing harmful poisons from your framework at all times. Toxins can get to be tricky to your wellbeing on the off chance that you accumulate enough of them to encounter cell malfunction.

There are numerous components that add to weight increase, and one element that is mostly ignored by customary eating methodologies is toxic overburden. All the more basically, individuals frequently experience issues getting in shape in light of the fact that their bodies are brimming with poisons. The more poisons you take in or get presented to consistently, the more poisons you store as fat cells in the body. Toxins that are stored in fat cells are hard to dispose of through abstaining from food alone. You should first detoxify the body.

At the point when the body is overloaded with poisons, it exchanges its vitality far from burning calories. Rather it uses that vitality to work harder to detoxify the body. As it were, the body does not have the vitality to burn calories. In any case, when the body is productively detoxifying and disposing of poisons, the vitality can be utilized to smolder fat.

The accompanying manifestations demonstrate the presence of overabundance poisons in the body: bloating, clogging, heartburn, low vitality, exhaustion/mind fog, melancholy, weight increase, perpetual agony, diseases, sensitivities, migraines, and gut/digestion issues.

Chapter 2: How To Do The 12-Day Green Smoothie Cleanse

The 12-Day Green Smoothie Cleanse is a really health-changing experience. You can do a full cleanse or a modified cleanse.

The full cleanse includes of three smoothies, snacks, and water/tea for the whole twelve days. This will give the most health and weight reduction advantages, with a normal weight reduction somewhere around ten and fifteen pounds.

The modified cleanse comprises of two green smoothies (one for breakfast and one for lunch), with one healthy meal for dinner, snacks, and water/tea. The one healthy meal a day may comprise of a salad of mixed greens, sautéed veggies, fish or chicken (flame broiled or prepared).

The modified cleanse is a decent plan with enormous medical advantages from the nutrient-rich smoothies.

Weight reduction may not be as dramatic, but rather you can hope to still lose somewhere around five and ten pounds in the twelve days. The modified cleanse was intended for those unwilling or not able to stay with the full cleanse for twelve days.

It is additionally amazing for the individuals who are not hoping to lose a considerable measure of weight but rather essentially detox. In case you're new to detoxing and need to gradually ease into the cleanse, this is an awesome choice.

For either cleanse, you will stay away from refined sugar, meat, milk, cheddar, alcohol, brew, espresso, soft drinks/diet soft drinks, prepared nourishments, fried foods and refined carbs (white bread, pasta, doughnuts, and so on.) amid the twelve days.

FULL CLEANSE:

DRINK SMOOTHIES:
Each day, drink at least three green smoothies; one for breakfast, lunch and supper. You can likewise sip on the smoothie for the duration of the day as you get hungry. It is essential to drink a smoothie or eat a little bit every three to four hours to keep your digestion system revved up.

Every smoothie ought to contain around 12 to 16 ounces of fluid. Essentially set up your whole day of green smoothies in the morning and pack it up to bring with you. Keep it refrigerated however much as could possibly carry.

EAT SNACKS:

You may snack on apples, celery, carrots, cucumbers, and other crunchy veggies that are engaging you for the duration of the day. Other high-protein snacks incorporate unsweetened peanut butter, hard-boiled eggs, and crude or unsalted nuts and seeds (handful).

Beverage WATER AND DETOX TEA:

Drink no less than eight glasses of water (64 ounces) every day, and beverage detox or herbal teas as fancied. Drink the detox tea first thing each morning as it helps the detox process by cleansing the detox organs—kidneys, liver, skin, and so on.

KEEP BOWELS MOVING?

Perform one of the two routines for colon cleansing to guarantee you have one to three bowel discharges for each day while detoxing.

5. Try not to EAT refined sugar, meat, milk, cheddar, alcohol, brew, espresso, soft drinks/diet soft drinks, processed food, refined carbs and fried food (white bread, pasta, doughnuts, and so on.)

Drink Smoothies And Eat One Healthy Meal:

Each day, drink two green smoothies for breakfast and lunch and eat one healthy meal for supper. The one healthy meal may comprise of a salad of mixed greens, sautéed veggies, and fish or chicken (flame broiled or heated). Any two suppers can be utilized for the green smoothies, the length of you just have one sound dinner for every day. Each smoothie ought to contain around 12 to 16 ounces of fluid. Essentially prepare your whole days' worth of green smoothies in the morning and pack it up to bring with you. Keep it refrigerated as much as could be allowed.

EAT SNACKS:
You may snack on apples, celery, carrots, cucumbers, and other crunchy veggies that are speaking to you for the duration of the day. Other high-protein snacks incorporate unsweetened peanut butter, hard-boiled eggs, and crude or unsalted nuts and seeds (just a modest bunch).

BEVERAGE WATER AND DETOX TEA:
 Drink no less than eight glasses of water (64 ounces) every day, what's more, drink detox or herbal teas as fancied. Drink the detox tea first thing each morning as it helps the detox process by purging the detox organs—kidneys, liver, skin, and so on.

KEEP BOWELS MOVING:
Perform one of the two techniques for colon cleansing to guarantee you to have one to three solid discharges for each day while detoxing.

5. Try not to EAT refined sugar, red meat, milk, cheddar, alcohol, brew, espresso, soft drinks/diet soft drinks, processed foods, fried foods, refined carbs (white bread, pasta, doughnuts, and so on)

CHAPTER 3: THE SHOPPING LIST

It is recommended that you buy veggies and fruits for the first five days in one go. There are two lists that are given to you to make the shopping experience easy for you. One list is for the first six days and the other is for the next six days of the cleanse.

3.1 FOOD FOR THE FIRST SIX DAYS

- 6 ounces of mango chunks
- 20 ounces frozen peaches
- 6 apples
- 1 bunch grapes
- 10 ounces froze mixed berries
- 20 ounces frozen blueberries
- 15 ounces frozen strawberries
- 1 bunch kale
- 20 ounces spring mix greens
- Bag of ground flaxseeds
- 3 bananas
- 20 ounces spinach
- Stevia sweetener (packets)

- Raw or unsalted nuts and seeds to snack on
- Vegetables and fruits of your choice to munch on
- Detox tea (by Triple Leaf or Yogi brands)
- Sea salt (or any iodized sea salt)
- OPTIONAL: Non-dairy/plant-based protein powder

3.2 Food For The Last Six Days

- 20 ounces froze mango chunks
- 20 ounces froze pineapple chunks
- 5 bananas
- 20 ounces frozen peaches
- 10 ounces froze mixed berries
- 2 apples
- 1 bunch kale
- 6 ounces frozen blueberries
- 6 ounces frozen strawberries
- 20 ounces spinach
- 20 ounces spring mix greens
- Fruit and veggies of your choice to munch on (such as apples, carrots, celery, etc)
- Raw or unsalted nuts and seeds to snack on

Chapter 4: Benefits Of A Smoothie Lifestyle

Since juice diets and a smoothie lifestyle is "what's in" these days, many people are starting to wonder if this particular lifestyle benefits them or not. Smoothies have picked up notoriety for being a blend created and is devoured basically by individuals who are health conscious. Although, carrying on with the "smoothie lifestyle" means more than simply drinking your vegetables and fruits. The fact of the matter is that having the capacity to make nutritious meals that you can intake through a straw is just the tip of the 'smoothie lifestyle' iceberg. Settling to healthy decisions during the entire day is what will determine how effective a health improvement program will be. This chapter explains how you can benefit if you adopt a smoothie lifestyle. Everyone knows that smoothies especially green are healthy. So what else?

Easy To Make And Are Portable

Smoothies are easy to make. All you need to do is blend in your favourite fruits and vegetables and drink the mixture. If you have a blender then making a green smoothie is the simplest thing to make. In addition, if these smoothies are kept cold and sealed, then these can stay fresh a day. If you use the perfect container, you can carry your smoothie everywhere with you.

Alkalizing & Detoxing

Smoothies are an extraordinary approach to detox your organs and alkalize the body. Since green smoothies are stuffed with chlorophyll, they can start detox by alkalizing our framework and free toxins we secure from the food we eat and from the environment. Initially, you may feel "off" from drinking green smoothies but this is essentially a minor reaction of the detox process.

Truth be told, once this passes, you will certainly feel better and more active than you have in years. Once more, this is a natural method of your body to attempt to dispose of poisons, and adding green smoothies to your eating routine is one of the most effortless (and mildest) methods for flushing out toxins.

Anti-Inflammatory

Green smoothies are extremely calming and have an anti-inflammatory effect on the grounds that the greens assist in mineralizing and alkalizing the body. This helps in getting rid of the toxic impact of an acidic eating routine. Devouring loads of processed foods high in saturated fats lead to an assortment of inflammation- related illnesses (like Arthritis, heart diseases and cancer). Dark leafy greens can help invert this impact.

They Help Prevent Kidney Stones

In spite of a couple of scare stories online that propose the oxalate levels in green leafy vegetables may harm your health, a study demonstrates that men taking a low-calcium diet endured double the rate of kidney stones contrasted with men eating a higher calcium diet. What contains a lot of dietary calcium? The top choice for a green smoothie, Kale has a high amount of calcium. It is believed that the calcium found in kale is ingested by the body easily as compared to the calcium in milk. In addition, its oxalate levels are low as well.

THEY FILL YOU UP

In case you're the kind of individual who feels hungry every thirty minutes, the additional fiber in a green smoothie could be the solution for your longing. What's more, in case you're on a diet, a green smoothie before your main course of the day will help you feel full and satisfied with smaller portions of food. Drinking plain water before a supper tops you off, however, the fiber plus fluid combination of a green smoothie works far better.

NATURAL WEIGHT LOSS

Numerous people have reported huge weight reduction by adding green smoothies to their eating routine. Green smoothies are high in vitamins, minerals and phytonutrients which signal to the cerebrum that the body is receiving good nutrition and does not require some other nourishment/food. Smoothies are likewise high in fiber and normally low in fat which helps people shed pounds rapidly and securely! Adding greens to your diet will adjust your hunger levels and dissipate your cravings.

CLEARER SKIN

Healthy eating, particularly when adding heaps of veggies and fruits, has been connected to much clearer, beautifully radiant skin. Smoothies are high in fiber, permitting the body to take out toxins through the liver, kidneys and colon rather than the skin. If the liver does not work properly and the colon is backed up then the body detoxes through the skin. Moving things through your body will eradicate this issue and permit your skin to glow and look fresh!

MENTAL CLARITY AND FOCUS

Supplanting your typical morning espresso rituals with green smoothies will offer you some assistance with feeling more alert, energetic, and diminish any anxious energy you may experience the ill effects of. Green smoothies permit the nerves to work at a speedier, effective rate on the grounds that they are high in B vitamins and potassium which sustains the nerves and the functioning of our mind.

CANCER PREVENTION AGENTS

Antioxidants and phytonutrients are very abundant in an appropriately prepared green smoothie. Antioxidants shield the body from infection and sickness and repair and prevent any DNA harm that originates from terrible free radicals. Cancer prevention agents and phytonutrients are likewise vital for vitality levels and guaranteeing you keep your body at ideal health and wellness.

EXPANDED ENERGY

Smoothies are pressed with vitamins and minerals and are processed effortlessly.easy digestion invites a lot of vitalities (contrasted with things that process slower and make you tired). Smoothies and clean eating likewise get out the colon, so the supplements in the nourishments you are eating are assimilated faster and provides the cells in your body with the vitality and energy they want and require.

THEY MAKE YOU SEXY

Last but not the least, it helps you look attractive. Some fruits and veggies have a circulation-enhancing effect which makes the individual look pretty and feel sexy.

4.1 WHAT ARE THE BEST GREENS FOR YOUR SMOOTHIE?

Now that you have committed to doing smoothies cleanse, you need to know which greens you should consume for your smoothies to bring out the best results.

Bok Choy: Bok choy is a Chinese cabbage that is crunchy and tastes well. It is brimming with vitamins A, C, and calcium, and, in addition, it has a lot of antioxidants.

Arugula: Arugula is a major source of folic acid as well as vitamins A, C, and K, and provides a boost for bone and brain health. Additionally it has a peppery flavour.

Collard Greens: Collards are green leafy vegetables that are nutritiously like kale yet chewier and with a much more grounded taste. They are better agents for binding to bile acids all through the digestive tract, which makes them great at bringing down cholesterol.

Beet Greens: Beet greens are the leafy tops to the beet vegetable. They are rich in vitamin K. They are known to enhance vision, avert Alzheimer's, and support the immune system.

Chard (otherwise known as Swiss Chard): Chard is a green leafy vegetable that shows red stalks, leaf veins, and stems. It has a beet-like taste and a gentle composition. It is known to avert tumors/cancers and is useful for purifying the digestive framework.

Dandelion Greens: Dandelion greens look like weeds in your grass, yet they are just another incredible wellspring of vitamins A and K. They help the digestion process some assistance with digesting and can help issues of constipation in light of the fact that they are a characteristic laxative.

Lettuce: Lettuce has been a mainstream staple in servings of mixed greens subsequent to the time of the Ancient Egyptians. It contains key amino acids and vitamins. Make certain to eat lettuces with dark green leaves to get the most astounding value of nutrition. Romaine lettuce, specifically, has abnormal amounts of vitamin C, K, and A and is a decent wellspring of folic acid.

Kale: Kale is lightweight with rough leaf edges. It is stacked with vitamins A, C, K, and that's only the tip of the iceberg. It is known for bringing down the dangers connected with creating prostate, ovary, breasts, colon, and bladder tumors.

Mustard Greens: Spicy mustard greens are successful in bringing down cholesterol and give a sound measurement of riboflavin, niacin, magnesium, and iron. They are a storage facility of phytonutrients that have numerous illness preventing properties.

Parsley: Parsley is rich in minerals, antioxidants, fibers and vitamins, and is known to help reduce aging and regulate blood sugar levels.

Turnip Greens: Turnip greens are slightly bitter but are full of flavour. Turnip greens are effective at providing various health benefits, but they stand out amongst other green leafy veggies in their ability to fight the development of cancerous cells.

Spinach: Perhaps the most beloved green leafy vegetable of them all, spinach is mild tasting and not as bitter as other greens. The dark green leaves of spinach really have a bunch of high levels of omega- 3s, magnesium calcium, and vitamins A, C, E, and K. When most people start drinking green smoothies, they start with spinach.

MILDER-TASTING GREENS:

- Butter lettuce
- Baby beet greens
- Kale
- Baby bokchoy
- Carrot top greens
- Spinach
- Romaine lettuce
- Swiss chard

STRONGER-TASTING GREENS:

- Mustard greens
- Arugula
- Dandelion greens
- Collard greens
- Radish tops
- Turnip greens
- Sorrel

- Watercress

Chapter 5: What To Include In Your Green Smoothie

For the 12-Days Green Smoothie Cleanse, the main adequate foods to include in your smoothies are green leafy vegetables and fruits. Do not include any starchy vegetables, for example, beets, sweet potatoes, carrots or whatever other vegetables those are not leafy greens. Fruit is typically processed rapidly, yet when it's blended with other bland vegetables, the stomach will let the organic product sit while it processes alternate foods that are in there.

The organic product will start to ferment which causes gas and bloating. To stay away from this, just include green leafy veggies, and fruits in the green smoothies amid the 12-day detox/cleanse.

Make certain to just utilize the darker assortments of green leafy vegetables as they give chlorophyll and other critical supplements. A few samples of leafy dark greens are kale, chard, spinach, a baby serving of mixed greens, beets greens, arugula, and collard greens romaine lettuce, and dandelion greens. It is essential to use organic products for the cleanse. If you can't find organic products then makes sure you wash off the waxes and pesticides as best as you can.

Waxes are really hard to evacuate; actually, they, as a rule, can't be uprooted by essentially washing them.

This is why you will have to buy cleaners from the market that are specially designed for this. You can also reduce the toxic content by scrubbing and soaking the veggies and fruits in 10% white vinegar and later washing it with water.

It is essential to utilize spring or sanitized water in your green smoothies. Another choice is alkaline water, which helps in detoxification and better hydration. Faucet water is not prescribed for use.

CHAPTER 6: POST CLEANSE

Planning a cleanse takes a lot of energy and time. Eventually, you come across the best cleanse program and you follow it and lose the desired amount of weight. Now, what? What you eat after the cleanse is as essential as what you eat during the cleanse. This is because if, after 12 days, you start eating like a maniac, you will obviously gain back the weight.

The way to end and break your cleanse is to do it gradually. Slowly, introduce your regular diet back into your life and eat moderately rather than large portions. Start by eating foods that are easy to digest which includes pureed or steamed veggies, or lightly sautéed greens, also you can intake proteins such as eggs, legumes, whey and nuts. You can also consume green soups that are made with pureed strings beans, celery and zucchini. This nourishes the body with natural sodium, electrolytes and potassium. For an extra boost, you can also intake cooked carrot.

If you want to have meat again then you should do it gradually. Rather than beef or fish, you need to consume organic poultry which can contain mercury. Whatever you eat, you need to eat smaller portions. People, during the detox, know that they cannot have a lot of portions so they eat less. Consuming smaller portions after the cleanse helps you realize how much you actually need to eat. Additionally, you need to drink green smoothie to feel filled and keep the detox going. Moreover, you can also have hot lemon water.

SAMPLE MEAL PLAN:

Breakfast- after the green smoothie cleanses, the first day you should have a fruit bowl for breakfast. If you do not want to have fruits, then you can always have a bowl of simple light salad with lemon juice dressing.

Lunch- Continue with a salad for lunch, and you might add fermented foods and sprouts here. These are pre-digested foods, which makes them easy to digest.

Dinner- For dinner has lightly steamed veggies mixed with lemon juice, dulse flakes and Himalayan sea salt. You can also have a raw vegetable soup and some cayenne pepper. Continue have light foods rather than larger portions.

The key is to consume light nourishments, no meat, refined sugar or dairy or wheat and they must be organic. You should not push your organs and tax your digestion by consuming overwhelming foods right away. Keep up your liquids. The smoothies should be a part of your regular diet.

On Day 3 keep on eating light suppers however you may begin to re-introduce nuts and seeds, for instance, breakfast could be some blended drenched nuts with soaked chia mixed to make morning breakfast porridge and include some homemade crude almond milk.

Include back in the good fats, for example, Coconut Oil, Avocado, Extra Virgin Olive Oil, Hemp Seed Oil or Flax Seed Oil. Include some gluten free grains, for example, Quinoa, Amaranth or Millet to your dinners.

On Day 4, keep on eating as above, however, you may add some light animal protein if you want to, for example, steamed fish, eggs and chicken. This is how you need to go about it, post cleanse.

Since you have done a 12-day green smoothie cleanse, this is a great chance to not slip once more into any bad eating habits of consuming wheat, meat, dairy or processed foods. You might even want to give up the coffee and alcohol as well. These are foods that are highly addictive and will suck you into the vicious cycle of cravings and eating larger portions.

Lastly, the most critical part is to praise yourself! What an immense accomplishment and really extraordinary approach to honour yourself for being brave enough to complete the 12 day green smoothie cleanse. Moreover, you will feel more energetic, healthier and stronger.

CHAPTER 7: ADDITIONAL INFORMATION

Having the same smoothie every day can get very monotonous and this is why this self-help guide brings you the most delicious recipes that you can drink during the 12-day green smoothie cleanse. Looking for recipes online can be tiring and you can lose motivation. That is why this book wants to keep you motivated and helps you by providing recipes.

Recipes:

Berry Peachy

- 2 handfuls kale
- 2 cups water
- 1½ cups froze peaches
- 1 handful spinach
- 2 apples, cored, quartered
- 2 packets stevia
- 1½ cups froze mixed berries
- 2 tablespoons ground flaxseeds
- OPTIONAL: 1 scoop of protein powder

Place leafy greens and water into the blender and blend until mixture is a green juice-like consistency. Stop the blender and add remaining ingredients. Blend until creamy.

Pineapple Spinach

- 2 cups fresh spinach, packed
- 2 bananas, peeled
- 1 cup pineapple chunks
- 1½ packets stevia
- 2 cups frozen peaches
- 2 tablespoons ground flaxseeds
- 2 cups water
- OPTIONAL: 1 scoop of protein powder
- Place spinach and water into the blender and blend until mixture is a green juice-like consistency. Stop blender and add remaining ingredients. Blend until creamy.

Peach Berry Spinach

- 3 handfuls spinach
- 1½ cups blueberries
- 2 cups water
- 1 handful fresh or frozen seedless grapes
- 1 cup froze peaches
- 2 tablespoons ground flaxseeds
- 3 packets stevia to sweeten
- OPTIONAL: 1 scoop of protein powder
- Place spinach and water into the blender and blend until mixture is a green juice-like consistency. Stop blender and add remaining ingredients. Blend until creamy.

PINEAPPLE BERRY

- 2 handfuls spring mix greens
- 1 banana, peeled
- 1½ cups froze mango chunks
- 2 handfuls spinach
- 1 ½ cups pineapple chunks
- 3 packets stevia
- 1 cup froze mixed berries
- 2 tablespoons ground flaxseeds
- 2 cups water
- OPTIONAL: 1 scoop of protein powder
- Place leafy greens and water into the blender and blend until mixture is a green juice-like consistency. Stop blender and add remaining ingredients. Blend until creamy.

Day 9: Apple Mango

- 3 handfuls spinach
- 1½ cups mangoes
- 2 cups water
- 1 apple, cored, quartered
- 2 tablespoons ground flaxseeds
- 2 cups frozen strawberries
- 1 packet stevia
- OPTIONAL: 1 scoop of protein powder
- Place spinach and water into the blender and blend until mixture is a green juice-like consistency. Stop blender and add remaining ingredients to blender. Blend until creamy.

Pineapple Kale

- 2 handfuls kale
- 2 cups water
- 1 handful spring mix greens
- 1½ cups froze peaches
- 2 packets stevia
- 2 handfuls pineapple chunks
- 2 tablespoons ground flaxseeds
- OPTIONAL: 1 scoop of protein powder
- Place leafy greens and water into the blender and blend until mixture is a green juice-like consistency.

Conclusion

You turn on the internet and you will surely bump into one of the green drinks. Yes, that's the one that just popped in your head. These green smoothies are viral all over the social media. This is because they have such varied benefits that I'm sure you are aware of now. Green smoothie cleanse is imperative as it brings back the energy that the pollutants and chemicals in the environment are eating up. This detox not only induces weight loss but also affects your emotions.

The more greens you intake, the happier your emotional state will be. Many greens have the ability to reduce the risk of cancers and also contribute to the decrease of depression and anxiety. Greens smoothies are anti-inflammatory which the basic requirement for us today is probably.

This 12- day green smoothie cleanse is more of a lifestyle that encourages you to make healthy choices throughout your life. Adding greens to the diet is advantageous to the health and this is why a green smoothie does wonders. Green smoothies are better than juices as they leave the pulp and the fibre in the smoothie for you to consume. These fibres will make you feel full and you would want to eat less, eventually leading to weight loss.

This program has shown amazing results over the 12 days that you follow this routine. This book guides you to follow a green smoothie cleanse for the best results ever. T talks about what vegetables and fruits would be best for your smoothies and why.

The great news about a smoothie cleanse is that you can be creative with it. You can add any of your favourite veggies and fruits to make the smoothie you crave for. You can add strawberries for extra flavour or any fruit that you like. It's delicious and it has great health benefits, so what more do you need?

PART 2

Introduction

It is easy to see why smoothies are gaining such popularity. Smoothies are soothing and invigorating and they are quite tasty and low in fat. Smoothies are also filling, portable, and quick -- all big pluses in our busy fast paced lives.

Smoothies can refresh and energize your nutrition-starved body. They are an easy way to pack a lot of fruits and vegetables into one meal or snack.

Don't give up, drinking smoothies to lose weight really works and you won't feel deprived like you are on a diet with smoothies. In fact, you will never feel hungry because smoothies are so filling and you will lose weight.

Now keep in mind, because their ingredients can vary, not all smoothies are created equal. To lose weight with smoothies you want to make sure your smoothies have a variety of healthy, all-natural, low fat ingredients.

There are plenty of healthy benefits of drinking smoothies. Blended smoothies are great for a concentrated nutritious meal that's ready in minutes. Depending on the ingredients you choose, smoothie recipes can be packed with protein, vitamins, and other nutrients. Smoothie recipes that promote weight loss are easy to find online and in many books.

You can accelerate your weight loss, boost your energy, enhance your health and improve your appearance all by adding healthy smoothies to your daily plan.

Discover the health benefits of smoothies in this cookbook packed with ease and tasty smoothie recipes for healthy living.

Let's get started!

Chapter 1: Home Prepared Smoothies

At home prepared smoothies are becoming more and more popular for everyone to add more fruits and vegetables to their diets.

With smoothies, you can easily get the recommended 5 daily servings of fruits and vegetables without the chore required if you were to eat the actual fruits and vegetables. At home smoothies when incorporated into your diet, will also allow you to lose weight quickly the healthy way.

Homemade smoothies are an excellent way to add fruits as well as certain types of yogurt which are superfoods because they are packed chock full with nutrients into your diet without the added calories.

It is important to note that a commercial smoothie may not be as beneficial for you because they will contain more calories and sugars than a homemade smoothie which will defeat your weight loss goals. A typical commercial smoothie size usually starts from 16 ounces up which is alot of calories.

You will be in a better position if you prepare the smoothies yourself and you will save money. It will usually take you less than two minutes to prepare one so you have no excuses.

If you have a family, preparing smoothies is also a great way for your children to consume the required fruits and vegetables which they will not otherwise consume without it being prepared in a smoothie which is not only healthy but also delicious. This is also a fun way to get them involved in the kitchen when you have various smoothie recipes.

The great thing about smoothies is that you shall be able to use the entire fruits and vegetables without discarding any nutrient rich parts. Unlike fruit juices, smoothies utilize the pulp of fruits and vegetables in the preparation. The pulp is an excellent source of fiber which helps you feel full quicker so that you consume less calories and lose weight quicker.

Smoothies will also allow your body to digest food and eliminate waste quicker and more efficiently and encourage the maintenance of good health. It is important to lose weight in a healthy manner and at home smoothies allow you to accomplish this goal.

Homemade smoothies can be created from a variety of healthy ingredients and almond milk or non dairy yogurt are great additions in order to create creamy smoothies. Use soy milk and use honey which is a natural sweetener instead of sugar or artificial sweeteners and watch your excess weight decrease when you step on a scale.

Leafy vegetables such as cabbage, carrots, celery, asparagus and even flowers such as broccoli and cauliflower are excellent for adding to smoothies for all the nutrients they contain that are great for the body as well as maintaining skin that will not be susceptible to premature aging and healthy hair and nails.

With all these benefits, how can you not start making smoothies on a daily basis? You can use smoothies as a snack or dessert. You can also use them as a meal replacement for faster weight loss.

If you have only a few minutes in the morning, having a smoothie for breakfast is an excellent option. The preparation time is minimal and you shall ensure that you have a healthy breakfast.

Breakfast is said to be the most important meal of the day, it shall boost your metabolism which allows for more calories to be burned in a day. Do not skip this meal if you would like to lose weight and having a smoothie at this time ensures that you kick start your metabolism early in the day even when you are pressed for time.

You can be as healthy or as indulgent as you would like with your at home prepared smoothies but it is important to add a variety of recipes so that you do not get bored with this smoothie habit.

CHAPTER 2: BENEFITS OF HEALTHY SMOOTHIE RECIPES

Healthy Smoothie Recipes can heal our internal systems thus promoting weight loss and increased energy. The secret to losing weight is found in nature. Fresh fruit and vegetables provide essential vitamins, minerals and nutrients necessary for optimal health. The combination of such has an impact on digestion, metabolism and absorption of these nutrients.

To lose weight, consider fruits and vegetables that have a lower energy density, meaning they have fewer calories (or energy) than their weight in grams. To calculate the energy density divide the calories of the food per serving with the weight of the food in grams per serving.

A low energy density is determined by the high water and fiber content of the raw food. Specifically, the water and fiber found in fresh produce allows us to experience the same level of feeling full as does a high calorie meal of unhealthy foods. Dieters can enjoy consuming a greater amount of food with lower energy density and still lose weight.

A way to achieve the best benefits from your healthy smoothie recipes is to consider the proper combination of fruits and vegetables. Certain foods may not be compatible with each other in terms of successful digestion.

For example, fruit digests rapidly. Fruit enters the stomach for a short period then travels to the intestines to digest in its own enzymes. This is in comparison to foods that are high in protein or carbohydrates.

If a healthy fruit smoothie is consumed directly following a meal which takes hours to digest, the potential for nutrient absorption can be lost. While the meal is being digested, the once clear path to the intestines is blocked.

The undigested matter can cause health problems such as weight gain and toxic activity. According to these principles, the time for healthy smoothie recipes is on an empty stomach.

The science of food combining can be extended to the classes of fruits and vegetables. Melons such as watermelon and cantaloupe are in a class by themselves in terms of rapid digestion. Use melons as the sole ingredient in a smoothie.

The sweet fruits including bananas, dates and persimmon do not contain as much water and tend to take longer to digest than acid fruits, sub-acid fruits and melons.

For optimum digestion, sweet fruits can be made into healthy smoothies without adding other fruits. Celery, spinach and lettuce are good ingredients to include with fruit in your smoothie. Maximum absorption of nutrients is the goal for health.

Chapter 3: Low Calorie Smoothies To Help You Lose Weight

If you are trying to lose weight, then one of the main things to watch out for is snacking. Everyone likes to have a delicious snack from time to time however, most snacks are fully of sugar and empty calories.

Even fat-free snacks are not healthy for you in excess. An alternative to unhealthy sugary snacks is making low calorie smoothies at home. All you really need is a blender or smoothie maker, fruit, yogurt, ice, and a bit of honey.

Low calorie smoothies can often be made using frozen fresh fruit. Smoothies of this nature are quite easy to make. You would first of all want to buy some of your favorite fruit-apples, bananas, strawberries, watermelon, peaches, plums- pretty much any fruit will do.

You then need to cut the fruit into pieces about the size of an ice cube and freeze it ready for use. Freezing fruit beforehand makes it even quicker to whizz up a low calorie snack when you feel hungry.

Another important ingredient in low fat low calorie smoothies is plain non dairy yogurt. This is yogurt that does not have any additional flavoring or sugar-check the ingredient list on the yogurt container to ensure that there are no added ingredients. This can be stored in your refrigerator or even frozen instead of the fruit.

The fruit and yogurt are then blended together. Many people add sugar to such a smoothie, but this is something that you should seriously consider avoiding. Most fruits are quite sweet on their own and you do not need much more sweetener added.

If you do want to add sweetener, then often a bit of honey is a good option. Sugar and low or no fat sugar substitutes and sweeteners should be avoided; most are not good for your health.

Smoothies can be part of your healthy eating plan even if you are at your healthy weight and are not trying to diet. Homemade smoothies are not only delicious they are also much healthier than commercial snacks and ice creams.

While the idea of a vegetable smoothie may sound gross, an avocado smoothie can actually be quite delicious. Avocado is actually technically a fruit; while it is not as sweet as most other fruits it can be turned into a delicious smoothie using a good recipe. Avocados are also full of important vitamins and minerals that are very good for your health.

You can make a smoothie using only one fruit, or you can experiment in combining two or more different fruits together to create new smoothie flavors. You will find that these low calorie smoothies are not only fun to make but will also help to boost your health.

Drinking smoothies is an enjoyable way of making sure you get enough fruits in your diet. Since fruits and vegetables should actually make up around 60% of a person's diet, you should feel free to indulge in these healthy snacks on a regular basis.

Chapter 4: How To Make A Healthy Drink With The Smoothie

BLENDERS

You can't make a smoothie without a blender or a food processor. Well, perhaps you can but it won't be easy. And because convenience and ease is one of the smoothie's selling points, you'll have to invest in a good blender if you want to enjoy a healthy smoothie.

A blender is necessary to break up and blend the fruits and other ingredients in a smoothie. This is something that a juicer cannot do. A juicer will allow you to get only the fruit or vegetable juice, leaving behind the fiber. You won't be able to incorporate the ice, non dairy milk, almond yogurt, protein powder and other smoothie ingredients.

If you are going to purchase a smoothie blender, think about the fruits and other ingredients that will go into your drink. Many fruits are small and soft and they can be easily blended. Some fruits are harder, like apples and pears.

Vegetables can also be tough on a blender. You must have an idea about what fruits and vegetables you will be using so that you can choose a suitable blender. If you want to add ice cubes, make sure your smoothie blender can handle it.

Your blender must be powerful enough to process the fruits and vegetables for your smoothies. If it's not strong enough, you may get large chunks of fruits instead of a creamy smoothie. Another thing to consider is the capacity of your blender. If you will be making large batches of healthy smoothies, you'll need a blender with a large flask.

The blender should be easy to clean. You should be able to take out the blades so that you can clean the equipment properly. Otherwise, you'll have smoothie residues left in the blender. Make sure the blender is safe to use. It should come with a warranty. You can purchase a good blender online or at your local appliance store.

There are many brands and models of blenders out there that you can use to make a healthy smoothie. Choosing the best one is a matter of personal preference. You also have to think about your budget.

A good quality, economical blender such as an Oster blender is suitable if you are just starting out. If you want to spring for a professional-grade blender, you may want to consider a VitaMix or BlendTec blender.

These two are powerful blenders and they can even crush ice cubes. Keep in mind that professional blenders are expensive so you may want to give it some thought before deciding on the best smoothie blender for your needs.

Chapter 5: Green Smoothie Recipes

There are many types of green smoothie recipes as there are people who want to enjoy a healthy living lifestyle. Due to the nature of green smoothies everyone can create their own recipe. It is only a question of combining various fruits and vegetables and blending them together.

You can get ready made smoothies to buy from the shop but it is very easy to make your own at home. All you need is a blender and a selection of your favourite fruits and vegetables. To make your smoothie taste better, select the fruits and vegetables that you like best and include some sweet fruits as well.

There are many suggestions of green smoothie recipes on the Internet today. This is because there are many different kinds of combinations of fruits and vegetables that you can turn into a smoothie.

One advantage of going on a smoothie diet is that you do not need to starve yourself.

Since vegetables are low in fat and carbohydrates you can eat as much as you like without having to worry about putting on weight. In order not to get tired of or get bored with the types of smoothies you eat, you will need to have a good selection of fruits and vegetables from which you can prepare different types of smoothies.

This will also ensure that you continue with your weight-loss program without giving up. Like any weight-loss program, you will need to combine your smoothie diets with an effective exercise plan.

Yes green smoothie recipes can help you lose weight because of its very nature. It can be filling and nutritious and you can have as much as you like at various times of the day.
This means you do not need to starve yourself to lose weight.

Research proves that Green Smoothies are one of the best ways to quickly lose weight. However, it can be tricky to consume green smoothie unless you have proven recipes.
Here are some easy to follow recipes of Green Smoothies that you can use.

1. MINT MOJITO GREEN SMOOTHIE

Ingredients:

- 1.5 cups of fresh spinach
- 1 large handful of fresh mint
- 3/4 cups of coconut water, or regular water
- Juice of 2 limes
- 3 teaspoons of hemp seeds
- 1 frozen or freshly chopped banana
- ice cubes (optional)
- 2 teaspoons of honey (optional) Directions:

Add the mint, spinach and coconut water (or regular water) into the NutriBullet together and blend until the mixture is smooth.

Add the hemp seeds, lime juice and banana into your juicer, you can also add in the honey and a few ice cubes if you'd like then blend until the mixture is smooth. Garnish the mixture with mint and lime.

2. Love Your Body Green Smoothie

Ingredients:

- handful of spinach
- handful of kale
- ¼ cup of fresh parsley
- 5 frozen strawberries
- ½ A LEMON
- ¼ sliced cucumbers
- 3 teaspoons of hemp seeds
- 1 cup of almond milk

Directions:

Combine all of your green vegetables and liquids into the NutriBullet, blend until the mixture is smooth. Adjust the speed and add in the remaining ingredients, blend unto the mixture is smooth.

3. AVOCADO GRAPEFRUIT GREEN SMOOTHIE

Ingredients:

- 1 med. frozen banana, chopped
- ½ med. peeled grapefruit, chopped
- ¼ med. peeled avocado
- 1 lg. handful kale and spinach
- 1 in. of ginger root
- 1 tsp. of wheatgrass powder, or of choice
- ½ cup of filtered water, or regular

Directions:

Gather all of the listed ingredients and combine in your juicer then blend the mixture until it is even.

4. KALE AIDE GREEN SMOOTHIE

Ingredients:

- Juice of 1 whole lemon
- 5 mini apples
- Lg. chuck of peeled ginger
- 3 teaspoons of hemp seeds
- 1 stalk of celery
- ¼ cup of chopped cucumbers
- ¼ cup of fresh parsley
- 4 stalks of de-stemmed kale
- 1 cup of water

Directions:

Combine all of the greens into the NutriBullet then pour in the liquids. Blend the mixture until it is smooth. Lastly, add in the remaining ingredients then blend until the entire mixture is smooth.

5. Apple Kale Green Smoothie

Ingredients:

- ½ AN APPLE

- 1 cup of de-stemmed kale

- ½ cup of frozen pineapple

- ½ of a fresh squeezed lemon, or 1 tsp. of lemon juice

- 1 cup of water

- 1 serving of Vega One French Vanilla

- Ice (optional) Directions:
Gather all of the ingredients and add them into your juicer. Blend the mixture until it is smooth.

6. Restorative Detox Green Smoothie

Ingredients:

- ½ of a grapefruit
- 1 cup of coconut water
- 8 fresh basil leaves Directions:

Add all of the ingredients into your juicer and blend until the mixture is smooth.

7. Holiday Detox Smoothie

Ingredients:

- 2 lg. peeled and quartered oranges
- 1 lg. quartered and cored apple
- 1 16oz. bottle of Kombucha, or apple juice
- 3 cups of fresh spinach

Directions:
Put the apples, kombucha (or apple juice) and oranges into the juicer. Blend the mixture on low until the fruit is even. Add in the spinach to the blended fruit and increase the speed to high then blend the mixture until it is even and creamy in texture.

Chapter 6: Easy And Tasty Smoothie Recipes For Healthy Living

Smoothies are first and foremost and excellent way to get healthy. They allow you to meet your daily recommended servings of fruits and vegetables that many people lack in their diets.

Smoothies allow you to create a drink using the entire fruits and vegetables without discarding much of the fruit or vegetables as you would do if you ate the fruit or vegetable itself.

Let's face it, eating the actual fruits and vegetables that we require on a daily basis can be a chore lead to a lot of waste. Developing a smoothie habit actually makes eating fruits and vegetables enjoyable and less of a chore. The smoothie is so smooth and creamy and is a real treat.

Smoothies while healthy and enjoyable can be used as a way to lose weight fast. When you make the smoothie yourself, you can control the ingredients and ensure that they are low calorie and low fat to ensure fast weight loss. Most smoothies sold by various businesses will not help you lose weight because the calorie and fat content is through the roof.

Breakfast is the most important meal of the day and it help to kick start your metabolism. Boosting your metabolism will help you burn more calories per day and lose weight. Most people are simply too busy to eat a healthy breakfast each morning and end up losing a valuable opportunity to boost their metabolism.

If you are trying to lose weight fast, a diet smoothie will function as a great healthy breakfast to kick start your metabolism. It is easy to prepare and may take less than two minutes and you can take it with you on the road if you are too busy to sit down and have breakfast.

A diet smoothie is definitely a great way to enable fast weight loss and you can use it to replace any other meal besides breakfast or use it as a healthy snack during the day. This will prevent you from snacking on chips, sweets and other foods that will not help you accomplish your weight loss goals.

Smoothies are primarily created using fruits and/or vegetables with milk or yogurt added. For a diet smoothie you can control the ingredients by choosing low fat milk or yogurt which will help you accomplish you weight loss goals in little time. Smoothies are also very filling so you will not be starving yourself even when you replace a meal with a smoothie.

In addition to milk or yogurt, you can add about a tablespoon of protein powder to ensure that the smoothie will take you through lunch without experiencing hunger pangs leading to bingeing. Finding the right ingredients to make the diet smoothie that will help you lose weight fast is important.

There are many recipes for diet smoothies that you can use. To maintain a smoothie habit, you need variety and the more recipes you have, the better you will stick to this program and achieve fast weight loss. In this chapter. I will be sharing with you 50 sweet smooth recipes for your weight loss journey.

1. PEANUT BUTTER AND JELLY PROTEIN SMOOTHIE

Ingredients:

- 1 cup mixed frozen berries
- 1-2 tablespoons all-natural peanut butter
- 1/4 cup vanilla protein powder
- 2 tablespoons rolled oats
- 1 cup milk, any kind

Directions:
Place all ingredients in a blender and mix until smooth.

2. Spinach Flax Protein Smoothie

Ingredients"

- 1 cup unsweetened almond milk (or any kind)
- 1 large handful of organic baby spinach, washed
- ¼ cup frozen mango chunks
- ¼ cup frozen pineapple
- ½ of a banana (fresh or frozen)
- 1 Tbsp flax meal (optional)
- 1 Tbsp chia seeds (optional) • 1 scoop vanilla protein powder (optional)

Directions:
Combine all ingredients into a blender

Blend until smooth

Pour into a glass & serve

3. Skinny Oreo Milkshake

Ingredients:

- 1 medium frozen banana
- 1 cup almond milk
- 3 oreo cookies
- 1 teaspoon truvia
- 1 teaspoon vanilla extract
- 1 scoop protein powder

Directions:

Blend all ingredients, except cookies, until completely smooth. Add the cookies and pulse quickly until broken up. Pour into a glass, top with vegan whip if desired.

4. Sunrise Smoothie

Ingredients:

- 1 cup organic frozen mixed berries
- 1 frozen banana
- 1 orange, peeled and segmented
- 4 - 6oz Vanilla Greek Yogurt Directions:

Combine all ingredients in a blender then blend until smooth.

5. Dark Chocolate Peppermint Protein Shake

Ingredients:

- 1 large banana, frozen
- 2-3 large ice cubes
- 1 cup non-dairy milk of choice
- 1 scoop Designer Whey Gourmet Chocolate Protein Powder
- 2 tablespoons cocoa powder
- Pinch of sea salt
- 1/4 tsp pure peppermint extract
- optional 1 tablespoon dark/vegan chocolate chips
- toppings: homemade whipping cream, vegan whipped topping, or Greek yogurt Directions:

Place all ingredients in a blender and blend until smooth. Enjoy

6. ALMOND BUTTER CHIA SMOOTHIE

Ingredients:

- 1 large ripe banana peeled and frozen
- 3/4 cup unsweetened almond milk
- 1 tablespoon unsweetened almond butter
- 1 tablespoon chia seeds Optional Add-ins:
- Ground cinnamon
- MACA POWDER
- raw cacao powder
- Blueberries or fruit of choice • Spinach or leafy green of choice Directions:

Put it all in a blender and blend until smooth.

7. HEALTHY COFFEE BANANA SMOOTHIE Ingredients:

- 1 cup chilled Seattle's Best brewed coffee
- 1 1/2 bananas, cut into chunks
- 1 cup nonfat plain Greek yogurt
- 1 tbsp ground flax seed
- 2 tsp honey or agave nectar
- 1/2 tsp ground cinnamon
- 1/4 tsp grated nutmeg

- 6 ice cubes Directions:

Place all of the ingredients in a heavy-duty blender (one that can crush ice).

Blend until smooth and Serve.

8. Grape And Blueberry Protein Smoothie

Ingredients:

- 1 tablespoon ground flax meal
- 1 ripe banana peeled and frozen
- 1/2 cup fresh blueberries
- 1/2 cup frozen red grapes
- 3 large ice cubes
- 1 cup unsweetened almond milk
- 1/4 cup orange juice
- 1/8 teaspoon to 1/4 ground cinnamon Directions: Add all ingredients for the smoothie to a blender and blend until completely smooth.

9. Berry Oat Breakfast Smoothie

Ingredients:

- ½ cup old fashioned rolled oats
- 1 cup almond milk (more as needed)
- ½ cup frozen berries
- 3 tablespoons honey (or to taste)
- ⅓ cup non dairy yogurt
- ¼ cup ice Directions:

Add all ingredients to a blender. Cover tightly and pulse until ice is broken up, then puree until smooth. Taste and add sweeter if needed or milk if it is too thick. Serve immediately.

10. Chocolate Peanut Butter Banana Breakfast Shake

Ingredients:

- 2 large overripe bananas , peeled, sliced and frozen
- 1 cup original almond milk (or more to thin as desired)
- 3/4 cup ice
- 1/4 cup creamy peanut butter
- 2 Tbsp unsweetened cocoa powder
- 1/2 tsp vanilla extract Directions:

Add all ingredients to a blender a process until well pureed. Serve immediately.

11. Blueberry Almond Butter Smoothie

Ingredients:

- 1 banana, peeled
- 1 cup frozen blueberrie1/2 cup almond butter
- 1/2 cup plain yogurt
- 3/4 cup almond milk
- 3 dates, pitted and quartered
- 1 cup ice, or as needed Directions:

Combine all ingredients in a blender; purée on high speed until smooth. Add a few ice cubes and blend until it reaches your desired consistency.

12. Raw Chocolate Smoothie

Ingredients:

- 1 tablespoon raw honey
- 1 medium banana
- 2 tablespoons raw peanut butter
- 1 1/2 tablespoons raw cacao powder
- 1/2 cup almond milk, either store-bought or homemade

Directions:

Optional: warm the raw honey to thin it out by running the jar under hot water.

Puree honey, banana, peanut butter, cacao and almond milk in a sturdy blender until smooth.

13. Raw Banana Bread Shake

Walnut milk ingredients:

- 1 cup raw walnuts, soaked for at least 4 hour
- 3 cups filtered water
- Raw banana bread shake ingredients
- 3 cups walnut milk
- 2 scant cups sliced bananas (fresh or frozen)
- 1 tsp ground cinnamon
- pinch of fresh grated nutmeg
- 1/2 tsp vanilla powder (or extract)
- 1 tbsp maple syrup (optional, but I enjoy it)
- Ice (optional)
- 2 tbsp cacao nibs

Directions:

Make the walnut milk: strain the soaked walnuts and place them in an upright blender. Add the filtered water to the blender. Blend the mixture on high for about 2 minutes, or until you have a fluid, creamy "milk." Strain the milk with a fine mesh strainer over a large bowl or pitcher.

Push the walnut pulp in the strainer with the back of a spoon to get all of the milk out. Pour the strained milk into a sealable container and refrigerate until ready to use. The milk will separate, so just shake it every time you use it.

For the shake: In an upright blender, combine the walnut milk, sliced bananas, cinnamon, nutmeg, vanilla powder and maple syrup (and ice, if using).

Blend on high until you have a creamy and smooth mixture. Add the cacao nibs and blend for 10 seconds more—just so that you have little cacao "chips" throughout the drink.

Pour the raw banana bread shake into glasses and garnish with toppings if you like.

14. Peach & Oat Breakfast Smoothie

Ingredients:

- 1 1/2 cups peeled and diced , frozen peaches
- 1 cup almond coconut milk blend or original almond milk
- 1 (5.3 oz) non dairy yogurt - mango, peach, strawberry or coconut
- 1 very ripe banana , peeled and frozen
- 1/2 cup oats (old fashioned or quick, either are fine)
- 1/2 cup cold water Directions:

Add all ingredients to a blender and process until well pureed. Serve immediately.

15. Carrot Cake Smoothies

Ingredients:

- 4 medium carrots, peeled and roughly chopped
- 9 ounces vanilla non dairy yogurt
- 1-1/2 cups unsweetened vanilla almond milk
- 1/4 cup plus 2 tablespoons toasted shredded coconut
- 1/4 cup plus 2 tablespoons walnuts
- 1 tablespoon honey
- 1/2 teaspoon ground cinnamon
- 1/4 teaspoon ground ginger
- 1/4 teaspoon ground nutmeg
- 1/2 cup ice (optional) Directions:

Combine all ingredients in blender until smooth. Serve immediately.

16. Apple Almond Flax Smoothie

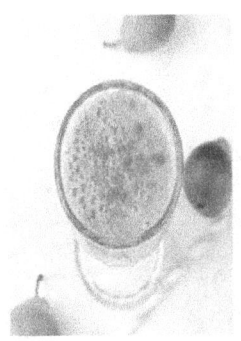

Ingredients:

- 1 large apple, cut into small pieces
- 1/2 frozen banana
- 1 tablespoon almond butter
- 1 tablespoon ground flaxseed
- 1/2 teaspoon cinnamon
- 1/2 cup coconut milk
- Optional: handful of kale

Directions:

Combine all the ingredients in a blender.

Puree until smooth and enjoy immediately

17. Avocado + Lime Green Tea Smoothie

Ingredients:

- Flesh from 1 avocado
- 2 sweet apples, cored and roughly chopped
- ½ small zucchini, roughly chopped
- ½ cup chopped broccoli florets
- 1 small knob peeled ginger
- Roughly ¼ cup loosely packed parsley
- ½ juiced lime
- 2 leaves kale
- 1 cup brewed + cooled green tea
- ⅔ cup almond milk (or water)

- 2 tsp chia seeds (optional) Directions:

Add all ingredients to a high-powered food processor and blend until smooth and combined.

Pour into two jars and stir a teaspoon of chia seeds through each. Allow to sit at least half an hour (though overnight is best) before consuming.

18. STRAWBERRY BEET SMOOTHIE

Ingredients:

- ½ cup coconut water
- 1 cup strawberries, chopped & frozen
- 1 banana, frozen
- 1 small/medium beet; scrubbed, ends trimmed, and roughly chopped*
- 1 T coconut oil

Directions:
Combine all ingredients in a blender, and blend on high until smooth and creamy for about 2 minutes. If you want a sweeter smoothie, add in a date or two, or a tablespoon of honey to taste.

19. Grapefruit Green Smoothie

Ingredients:

- 1 grapefruit, peeled, seeds removed (reserve juice)
- 1 large sweet apple, cored and skin removed
- 2 cups spinach
- 1 large ripe banana, previously sliced and frozen
- 2-3 ice cubes
- Unsweetened almond milk, water, or orange juice to thin (~1/2 cup)
- optional: 1/2 tsp fresh ginger, peeled and chopped

Directions:
Add all ingredients to a blender (including reserved grapefruit juice) and blend until creamy and smooth.

Add more liquid if too thick, ice to thicken, and banana or apple to sweeten.

20. CLEMENTINE SUNSHINE SMOOTHIE

Ingredients:

- 4 clementines, preferably chilled
- ½ CUP ICE
- ¼ cup yogurt or almond milk (plain or vanilla flavors work)
- Tiny dash sea salt
- Chunks of frozen banana for extra creaminess (you can scale back on the ice if using frozen banana)
- ¼ teaspoon ground turmeric for exotic flavor and more immunity-boosting properties
- Drizzle of honey for extra sweetness

- One drop of pure vanilla extract for more of a dreamsicle flavor

Directions:

Use your fingers to peel the clementines and pull each one in half. Pull out any excess pith in the center and discard it.

Add the yogurt or almond milk to the blender, followed by the clementines, ice and a tiny dash of salt, which enhances the other flavors. Feel free to add any of the optional add-ins suggested above. Blend well, until the clementines have turned into juice and there are no chunks of ice left.

There will probably still be some bits of pith in the smoothie. If you don't mind some texture, pour into a glass and enjoy immediately. For a perfectly smooth smoothie, pour it through a metal sieve into your glass.

21. Key Lime Pie Breakfast Smoothie

Ingredients:

- 1 container (6 ounces) key lime pie yogurt
- 1 cup unsweetened almond milk or sub another milk
- 1 large banana frozen
- 1 (~1 cup) ripe mango frozen
- 1/2 teaspoon vanilla extract
- 1 teaspoon truvia or sub another sweetener
- 1 tablespoon freshly squeezed lime juice
- (~1/3 cup) Small handful spinach
- Optional: 1/4 teaspoon xanthan gum makes it thicker
- Optional garnish: 1 graham cracker, reduced-fat whipped topping Directions:

Before making this smoothie, have a banana peeled, coined, and frozen. Also peel and remove the pit of the mango. Chop into pieces and freeze.

In a blender, combine the yogurt, milk, frozen banana, frozen mango, vanilla extract, sweetener of choice, lime juice, and spinach. (Increase spinach amounts of desired) If desired add in the xanthan gum.
Blend until completely smooth.

Optionally garnish with whipped topping and a few graham cracker crumbs

22. Matcha Mint Chip Smoothie

Ingredients:

- 1 ripe banana, frozen
- 1 tablespoon matcha
- 1 tablespoon chia seeds
- ½ avocado
- 1-2 sprigs of fresh mint
- A big handful of spinach
- 1 cup vanilla almond milk, unsweetened

- 1 heaping tablespoon cacao nibs Directions:
Combine all the ingredients, except for the cacao nibs, in a blender and blend until smooth and creamy. Add in the cacao nibs and blend for one second more. Pour into a glass and enjoy.

23. Healthy Peanut Butter Cup Smoothie

Ingredients:

Peanut Butter Layer

- 1 medium banana, frozen
- 1/4 cup peanut flour OR 2 tablespoons peanut butter
- pinch of salt
- 1/2 teaspoon vanilla extract
- 1 cup Unsweetened Silk Almond Milk
- 4 large ice cubes

Chocolate Layer

- 1 medium banana, frozen
- 3 tablespoons cocoa powder
- handful of spinach

- 1 cup Unsweetened Silk Almond Milk

Peanut Butter Layer

Place all ingredients in a blender or magic bullet. Mix until smooth.

Chocolate Layer

Place all ingredients in a blender or magic bullet. Mix until smooth.

24. Kale-Ginger Detox Smoothie

Ingredients:

- 1 ripe banana, peeled and frozen
- ½ cup frozen blueberries
- 2 teaspoons ginger, peeled and finely grated
- 2 cups kale leaves, loosely packed
- 1 cup unsweetened almond milk
- 1 tablespoon chia seeds (optional)
- 1/8 teaspoon ground cinnamon
- 2 teaspoons to 1 tablespoon raw honey

Directions: Add all ingredients to a blender and blend until completely smooth. If necessary, add more almond milk to help your blender process the frozen fruit.

25. Blueberry Coconut Lime Smoothie

Ingredients:

- 1 large banana frozen beforehand

- 1 container (5.3 ounces) • 1 cup almond milk
- 1 cup frozen blueberries

- 2 tablespoons unsweetened flaked coconut

- 2 tablespoons raw almonds

- 1/2 teaspoon truvia or sub another sweetener

Peel the banana and slice into coins. Place the coins in a sealed bag in the freezer the night before making this smoothie.

Combine the Key Lime Greek yogurt, almond milk, frozen blueberries, frozen banana, unsweetened coconut, almonds, and sweetener in a large blender.

Blend until smooth and enjoy immediately.

26. Green Apple Pie Smoothie

Ingredients:

- 1 large Granny Smith apple, cored and cut into cubes
- 1 cup baby spinach
- 1 (12-ounce) package Mori-Nu soft silken tofu, chilled
- 1 tablespoon pure maple syrup, or to taste
- 1/2 teaspoon vanilla extract
- 1/2 teaspoon ground cinnamon
- Pinch of ground cardamom

Directions:
Place all of the ingredients into a blender and puree until smooth. Stop the blender and scrape down sides of blender as needed. The smoothie will be extra thick and creamy.

Pour into a glass (or divide between two glasses) and serve.

27. Kiwi Basil Smoothie

Ingredients:

- 3 frozen kiwis (freeze in small cubes for easy blending.
- 1 BANANA
- 1 pink grapefruit, juiced (about 3/4 cup juice)
- 1 Tbsp agave syrup
- small handful of fresh basil
- handful of ice cubes

Blend. Pour. Serve.

28. Vanilla Date Smoothie

Ingredients:

- 1 cup unsweetened almond milk

- 1 scoop vanilla protein powder, optional

- 1 large frozen banana

- 4 – 5 ice cubes or another frozen banana

- 3 – 4 medjool dates, pitted (soft and fresh is best)

- 1 teaspoon vanilla extract Directions:
Combine ingredients in blender and blend until smooth, about two minutes. Add a splash or two of extra almond milk if needed.

You may have visually small pieces of dates within the shake. That's ok, and even with those I had no trouble using my straw without having to clear the bottom of it maybe once or twice.

29. Superfood Power Smoothie

Ingredients:

- 2 large bananas, previously peeled, sliced, and frozen

- 1 heaping handful spinach (about 1.5 cups)

- 1/2 of a large apple, chopped

- 1/2 cup almond milk

- optional: 1 Tablespoon ground flax

- 7 large strawberries, sliced Directions:
Make sure you have a strong, powerful blender that will blend up the frozen banana and apple.

Peel the apple if you do not prefer the skin to be in your smoothie. I did not peel mine. Blend 1 banana, the spinach, apple, 1/4 cup almond milk, and flax together until smooth. Add more milk if it is too thick. Scrape down the sides of the blender as needed. Pour equally into 2 glasses.

Rinse out the blender and blend 1 banana, 1/4 cup almond milk, and the strawberries together until smooth. Scrape down the sides of the blender as needed and add more milk if it is too thick. Pour the strawberry smoothie on top. Serve immediately.

The layered smoothie look is optional, so you can just blend all of the ingredients together instead.

30. Raspberry Cheesecake Smoothie

Ingredients:

- 1 c. Greek vanilla yogurt
- 1 c. frozen raspberries
- 1/2 c. vanilla soy milk
- 1 frozen banana

- 2 oz. cream cheese Directions:

Combine all ingredients in a blender and mix until smooth.

31. Chocolate Covered Cherry Protein Smoothie

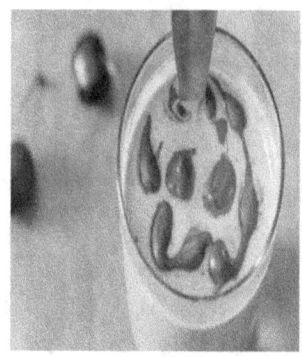

Ingredients:

- 1 and 1/2 large bananas, cut into chunks & frozen
- 6 oz Chobani Black Cherry Nonfat Yogurt
- 1/2 cup frozen cherries
- 1/3 cup milk

- 2 Tablespoons chocolate syrup Directions:

Make sure you have a strong, powerful blender that will blend up the frozen banana.

Add first 4 ingredients to blender. Blend until you've reached a smooth consistency. If desired, add more milk for a thinner smoothie.

Instead of chocolate syrup, try adding 1 Tablespoon of unsweetened cocoa powder or 1 Tablespoon of mini chocolate chips.

32. Chai Gingerbread Smoothie

Ingredients:

- 1½ frozen bananas
- ½ cup unsweetened organic vanilla almond milk (or other non-dairy milk)
- 1 handful of spinach
- 1 scoop of Vega Chai Protein Powder
- 1 tablespoon unsulphured blackstrap molasses
- 1 teaspoon vanilla extract
- ½ teaspoon ground cinnamon
- ½ teaspoon ground ginger

- Pinch himalayan of pink sea salt

Directions:

Place all ingredients into a high powered blender and blend until smooth

33. Cinnamon Roll Smoothie

Ingredients:

- 1 cup vanilla almond milk
- 1/2 cup vanilla Greek yogurt
- 1/4 cup old fashioned oats
- 1 Tablespoon brown sugar
- 1/4 teaspoon cinnamon (or 2-3 drops of Cinnamon Bark Essential Oil)

- 1 frozen banana (or fresh banana, but add in 3-4 ice cubes with fresh) Directions:

Place all ingredients in a blender and blend until smooth.

34. Apple Cinnamon Blueberry Smoothie

Ingredients:

- Large handful of baby spinach

- 1 cup frozen blueberries

- One 5.3 oz container Silk Blueberry Dairy-Free Yogurt Alternative or Blueberry Greek yogurt (can use plain but you may need to add additional syrup or other sweetener.

- 1 teaspoon pure maple syrup

- 1 teaspoon cinnamon

- 1 cup Silk Unsweetened Vanilla Almond milk or your milk of choice

- Ice cubes I used about four small ice cubes Directions:

Add all of the ingredients except the ice to your blender and blend until smooth.

Add ice and blend to achieve desired consistency.

35. Eggnog Smoothie

Ingredients:

- 1 cup Silk Unsweetened Cashew Milk
- 2 frozen bananas
- 2 pitted Mejool dates
- 1/4 cup plain Greek yogurt
- 1/2 teaspoon ground cinnamon
- 1/2 teaspoon ground nutmeg, plus additional for topping as desired
- 1/2 teaspoon almond extract
- Bourbon, rum, or whiskey (optional)

- Whipped topping (optional) Directions:

Place the cashew milk, banana, dates, Greek yogurt, cinnamon, nutmeg, and almond extract in a blender.

Puree until smooth. If desired, blend in rum, bourbon, or whiskey.

Pour into serving glass and top with whipped topping and additional nutmeg.

Kombucha and Spinach Smoothie

This recipe can be ready in 5 minutes, makes 1 serving (24 oz.), and will take approximately 45 seconds of blending assuming you are using a blender that is 1000 watts.

Nutrition Information
334 calories
22 g of fat
10 g of fat (saturated)
35 g of carbs
187 mg of sodium
10 g of fiber
18 g of sugar
3 g of protein

Ingredients

- Kale (1 c)
- Coconut oil (.5 T)
- Kombucha (1 c)
- Frozen papaya (.5 c)
- Cinnamon (.5 tsp)
- Spinach (1 c)
- Honey (.5 T)
- Flax seed (1 T)

- Ginger (2 tsp)

CAYENNE AND ARUGULA SMOOTHIE

THIS RECIPE CAN BE READY IN 5 MINUTES, MAKES 1 SERVING (24 OZ.), AND WILL TAKE APPROXIMATELY 45 SECONDS OF BLENDING ASSUMING YOU ARE USING A BLENDER THAT IS 1000 WATTS.

Nutrition Information
260 calories
2 g of fat
0 g of fat (saturated)
50 g of carbs
50 mg of sodium
13 g of fiber
30 g of sugar
4 g of protein

INGREDIENTS

- Maca (.5 T)
- Flax seed (1 T ground)
- Cayenne pepper (.25 tsp)
- Pear (1 halved)
- Honey (.5 tsp)
- Green apple (1 cored)

- Arugula (.5 c)
- Ginger (.5 tsp)
- Kale (1 c)
- Dandelion greens (1 c)
- Water (1 c)
- Lemon juice (.5 c)

Spicy Hot Smoothie

This recipe can be ready in 5 minutes, makes 1 serving (24 oz.), and will take approximately 45 seconds of blending assuming you are using a blender that is 1000 watts.

Nutrition Information
340 calories
24 g of fat
0 g of fat (saturated)
32 g of carbs
175 mg of sodium
12 g of fiber
15 g of sugar
5 g of protein

Ingredients

- Water (1 c)
- Kale (1 c)
- Frozen blueberries (.5 c)
- Avocado (.5 peeled)
- Coconut oil (.5 T)
- Chia seeds (1 T)
- Honey (.5 T)
- Chili powder (.25 tsp)

- Protein powder (20 g)
- Coconut flakes (1 T)
- Plain Greek yoghurt (.25 c)
- Maca (1 T)

Flax Seed and Kale Smoothie

This recipe can be ready in 5 minutes, makes 1 serving (24 oz.), and will take approximately 45 seconds of blending assuming you are using a blender that is 1000 watts.

Nutrition Information
275 calories
13 g of fat
5 g of fat (saturated)
40 g of carbs
285 mg of sodium
13 g of fiber
17 g of sugar
6 g of protein

Ingredients

- Frozen banana (1 peeled)
- Coconut oil (.5 T)
- Almond milk (1 c)
- Kale (1 c)
- Cinnamon (.25 tsp)
- Coconut flakes (1 T)
- Honey (.5 T)
- Flax seed (1 T)

- Protein powder (20 g)

CACAO AND AVOCADO SMOOTHIE

THIS RECIPE CAN BE READY IN 5 MINUTES, MAKES 1 SERVING (24 OZ.), AND WILL TAKE APPROXIMATELY 45 SECONDS OF BLENDING ASSUMING YOU ARE USING A BLENDER THAT IS 1000 WATTS.

Nutrition Information
260 calories
15 g of fat
3 g of fat (saturated)
30 g of carbs
400 mg of sodium
9 g of fiber
17 g of sugar
7 g of protein

INGREDIENTS

- Spirulina powder (1 T)
- Water (1 c)
- Spinach (1 c)
- Avocado (.5 peeled)
- Cinnamon (.25 tsp)
- Cacao powder (.5 T)

- Honey (.5 T)
- Pink Himalayan salt (1 tsp)
- Flax seed (1 T)
- Maca (.5 T)
- Protein powder (20 g)

WATERMELON AND TURMERIC SMOOTHIE

THIS RECIPE CAN BE READY IN 5 MINUTES, MAKES 1 SERVING (24 OZ.), AND WILL TAKE APPROXIMATELY 45 SECONDS OF BLENDING ASSUMING YOU ARE USING A BLENDER THAT IS 1000 WATTS.

Nutrition Information
182 calories
1 gram of fat
0 g of fat (saturated)
45 g of carbs
285 mg of sodium
13 g of fiber
25 g of sugar
4 g of protein

INGREDIENTS

- Frozen banana (1 peeled)
- Dandelion greens (1 c chopped)
- Water (.5 c)
- Watermelon (1 cup fresh)
- Cinnamon (.25 tsp)
- Honey (.5 T)
- Line juice (.5 lime)
- Ginger (.5 T)

- Turmeric (.5 tsp)
- Lemon juice (.5 lemons)

DANDELION AND BANANA SMOOTHIE

THIS RECIPE CAN BE READY IN 5 MINUTES, MAKES 1 SERVING (24 OZ.), AND WILL TAKE APPROXIMATELY 45 SECONDS OF BLENDING ASSUMING YOU ARE USING A BLENDER THAT IS 1000 WATTS.

Nutrition Information
230 calories
1 gram of fat
0 g of fat (saturated)
59 g of carbs
55 mg of sodium
10 g of fiber
34 g of sugar
3 g of protein

INGREDIENTS

- Chia seeds (1 T)
- Coconut oil (1 tsp)
- Spinach (.5 c)
- Coconut flakes (1 T)
- Water (1 c)

- Lemon (.5)
- Frozen banana (1 peeled)
- Red apple (1 cored)
- Dandelion greens (.5 c)

Green Tea and Spinach Smoothie

This recipe can be ready in 5 minutes, makes 1 serving (24 oz.), and will take approximately 45 seconds of blending assuming you are using a blender that is 1000 watts.

Nutrition Information
175 calories
5 g of fat
0 g of fat (saturated)
34 g of carbs
76 mg of sodium
4 g of fiber
20 g of sugar
15 g of protein

Ingredients

- Frozen banana (1 peeled)
- Baby spinach (1 c)
- Brewed green tea (1 cup)
- Honey (1 tsp)
- Protein powder (20 g)
- Honey (1 tsp)

Strawberry Arugula Smoothie

This recipe can be ready in 5 minutes, makes 1 serving (24 oz.), and will take approximately 45 seconds of blending assuming you are using a blender that is 1000 watts.

Nutrition Information
174 calories
5 g of fat
0 g of fat (saturated)
33 g of carbs
133 mg of sodium
5 g of fiber
18 g of sugar
2 g of protein

Ingredients

- Frozen banana (1 peeled)
- Arugula (.5 c)
- Frozen strawberries (1 c)
- Water (1 c)
- Spinach (.5 c)
- Sea salt (1 tsp)
- Honey (.5 T)
- Coconut oil (1 tsp)

Kale and Lime Smoothie

This recipe can be ready in 5 minutes, makes 1 serving (24 oz.), and will take approximately 45 seconds of blending assuming you are using a blender that is 1000 watts.

Nutrition Information
191 calories
1 g of fat
0 g of fat (saturated)
50 g of carbs
35 mg of sodium
5 g of fiber
30 g of sugar
3 g of protein

Ingredients

- Lemon (.5 peeled)
- Frozen banana (1 peeled)
- Ginger (.25 inch)
- Water (1 c)
- Pink Himalayan salt (1 tsp)
- Lime (.5 peeled)
- Kale (1 c)
- Honey (1 T)

MANGO AND AVOCADO SMOOTHIE

THIS RECIPE CAN BE READY IN 5 MINUTES, MAKES 1 SERVING (24 OZ.), AND WILL TAKE APPROXIMATELY 45 SECONDS OF BLENDING ASSUMING YOU ARE USING A BLENDER THAT IS 1000 WATTS.

Nutrition Information
240 calories
15 g of fat
3 g of fat (saturated)
30 g of carbs
285 mg of sodium
10 g of fiber
16 g of sugar
3 g of protein

INGREDIENTS

- Frozen mango (.5 c)
- Spinach (.5 c)
- Honey (.5 T)
- Cinnamon (.5 tsp)
- Flax seed (1 T)
- Avocado (.5 peeled)
- Frozen blueberries (.5 cups)
- Arugula (.5 c)

- Kale (.5 cups)

DANDELION GREENS AND MIXED BERRY SMOOTHIE

THIS RECIPE CAN BE READY IN 5 MINUTES, MAKES 1 SERVING (24 OZ.), AND WILL TAKE APPROXIMATELY 45 SECONDS OF BLENDING ASSUMING YOU ARE USING A BLENDER THAT IS 1000 WATTS.

Nutrition Information
270 calories
15 g of fat
9 g of fat (saturated)
36 g of carbs
75 mg of sodium
7 g of fiber
19 g of sugar
18 g of protein

INGREDIENTS

- Honey (.5 T)
- Frozen blackberries (1 c)
- Coconut oil (1 T)
- Flax seed (1 T)
- Frozen banana (1 peeled)
- Cinnamon (.25 tsp)

- Coconut oil (1 T)
- Water (1 c)
- Dandelion greens (1 c)

Baby Spinach and Pear Smoothie

This recipe can be ready in 5 minutes, makes 1 serving (24 oz.), and will take approximately 45 seconds of blending assuming you are using a blender that is 1000 watts.

Nutrition Information
222 calories
8 g of fat
0 g of fat (saturated)
39 g of carbs
24 mg of sodium
8 g of fiber
26 g of sugar
3 g of protein

Ingredients

- Pear (1 peeled)
- Flax seed (1 T)
- Baby spinach (1 c)
- Water (1 c)

- Ginger (.5 tsp)
- Honey (.5 T)
- Water (1 c)
- Flax seed (1 T)

Spicy Spinach Smoothie

This recipe can be ready in 5 minutes, makes 1 serving (24 oz.), and will take approximately 45 seconds of blending assuming you are using a blender that is 1000 watts.

Nutrition Information
170 calories
8 g of fat
1 g of fat (saturated)
28 g of carbs
300 mg of sodium
4 g of fiber
15 g of sugar
2 g of protein

Ingredients

- Frozen banana (1 peeled)
- Coconut oil (.5 T)
- Honey (.5 T)

- Chili powder (.25 tsp)
- Water (1 c)
- Spinach (1 c)
- Cayenne pepper (.25 tsp)
- Flax seed (1 T)

ROMAINE LETTUCE AND GINGER SMOOTHIE

This recipe can be ready in 5 minutes, makes 1 serving (32 oz.), and will take approximately 45 seconds of blending assuming you are using a blender that is 1000 watts.

Nutrition Information
135 calories
4 g of fat
0 g of fat (saturated)
60 g of carbs
85 mg of sodium
1 g of fiber
24 g of sugar
9 g of protein

INGREDIENTS

- Romaine lettuce (3 c)
- Ginger (.25 inches)

- Frozen mango (1 pitted)
- Lemons (2 peeled)
- Chia seeds (2 T)
- Spinach (2 c)
- Water (1 c)

Radish and Greens Smoothie

This recipe can be ready in 5 minutes, makes 1 serving (32 oz.), and will take approximately 45 seconds of blending assuming you are using a blender that is 1000 watts.

Nutrition Information
373 calories
2 g of fat
0 g of fat (saturated)
60 g of carbs
35 mg of sodium
15 g of fiber
16 g of sugar
6 g of protein

Ingredients

- Tangerines (2 peeled)
- Radish greens (1.5 c)

- Water (1 c)
- Red apple (1 cored)
- Dandelion greens (1 c)
- Ginger (.5 tsp)

CHARD AND BANANA SMOOTHIE

THIS RECIPE CAN BE READY IN 5 MINUTES, MAKES 1 SERVING (24 OZ.), AND WILL TAKE APPROXIMATELY 45 SECONDS OF BLENDING ASSUMING YOU ARE USING A BLENDER THAT IS 1000 WATTS.

Nutrition Information
200 calories
13 g of fat
2 g of fat (saturated)
35 g of carbs
109 mg of sodium
8 g of fiber
22 g of sugar
10 g of protein

INGREDIENTS

- Frozen banana (1 peeled)
- Almond butter (1 T)
- Mixed greens (2 c)
- Almond milk (.5 cups)

Kiwi Celery Smoothie

This recipe can be ready in 5 minutes, makes 1 serving (24 oz.), and will take approximately 45 seconds of blending assuming you are using a blender that is 1000 watts.

Nutrition Information
150 calories
9 g of fat
0 g of fat (saturated)
45 g of carbs
67 mg of sodium
15 g of fiber
22 g of sugar
11 g of protein

Ingredients

- Spinach (2 c)
- Pineapple (.25 cups)
- Kiwi (1 peeled)
- Water (1 c)
- Celery (2 stalks)
- Frozen banana (1)

SPINACH AND MIXED BERRY SMOOTHIE

THIS RECIPE CAN BE READY IN 5 MINUTES, MAKES 1 SERVING (24 OZ.), AND WILL TAKE APPROXIMATELY 45 SECONDS OF BLENDING ASSUMING YOU ARE USING A BLENDER THAT IS 1000 WATTS.

Nutrition Information
275 calories
13 g of fat
5 g of fat (saturated)
40 g of carbs
285 mg of sodium
13 g of fiber
17 g of sugar
6 g of protein

INGREDIENTS

- Spinach (2 c)
- Red apple (1 cored)
- Almond milk (1 c)
- Mixed berries (1 c)

BANANA, SPINACH AND PINEAPPLE SMOOTHIE

THIS RECIPE CAN BE READY IN 5 MINUTES, MAKES 1 SERVING (24 OZ.), AND WILL TAKE APPROXIMATELY 45 SECONDS OF BLENDING ASSUMING YOU ARE USING A BLENDER THAT IS 1000 WATTS.

Nutrition Information
300 calories
12 g of fat
2 g of fat (saturated)
22 g of carbs
189 mg of sodium
16 g of fiber
28 g of sugar
11 g of protein

INGREDIENTS

- Spinach (2 c)
- Frozen banana (1 peeled)
- Green apple (1 cored)
- Pineapple (1 c)
- Water (1 c)

CHARD AND COCONUT SMOOTHIE

THIS RECIPE CAN BE READY IN 5 MINUTES, MAKES 1 SERVING (24 OZ.), AND WILL TAKE APPROXIMATELY 45 SECONDS OF BLENDING ASSUMING YOU ARE USING A BLENDER THAT IS 1000 WATTS.

Nutrition Information
375 calories
12 g of protein
11 g of fat
4 g of fat (saturated)
28 g of carbs
23 g of sugar
9 g of fiber
54 mg of sodium

INGREDIENTS

- Chard (1 c)
- Plain yoghurt (1 c)
- Frozen strawberries (1 c)
- Frozen banana (1 peeled)

Weight loss smoothies

HIGH PROTEIN PEAR SMOOTHIE

THIS RECIPE CAN BE READY IN 5 MINUTES, MAKES 1 SERVING (24 OZ.), AND WILL TAKE APPROXIMATELY 45 SECONDS OF BLENDING ASSUMING YOU ARE USING A BLENDER THAT IS 1000 WATTS.

Nutrition Information
299 calories
9 g of fiber
27 g of protein
37 g of carbs
595 mg of sodium
6 g of fat
2 g of fat (saturated)
27 g of sugar

INGREDIENTS

- Almond milk (1 c)
- Spinach (1 c)
- Protein powder (20 g)
- Pear (1 cored)
- Matcha tea (.5 tsp)

Orange Smoothie with Spinach

This recipe can be ready in 5 minutes, makes 1 serving (24 oz.), and will take approximately 45 seconds of blending assuming you are using a blender that is 1000 watts.

Nutrition Information
146 calories
36 g of carbs
3 g of fat
25 g of sugar
100 mg of sodium
4 g of protein
6 g of fiber
0 g of fat (saturated)

Ingredients

- Spinach (1 c tightly packed)
- Navel orange (1 peeled)
- Banana (.5 peeled)
- Coconut water (.25 c)
- Ice cubes (6)
- Hemp seed (1 T)

Orange Protein Smoothie with Kale

This recipe can be ready in 5 minutes, makes 1 serving (24 oz.), and will take approximately 45 seconds of blending assuming you are using a blender that is 1000 watts.

Nutrition Information
300 calories
23 g of sugar
7 g of fiber
613 mg of sodium
35 g of carbs
2 g of fat (saturated)
6 g of fat
30 g of protein

Ingredients

- Water (1 c)
- Kale (1 c chopped)
- Protein powder (20 g)
- Spirulina powder (.5 tsp.)
- Navel orange (1 peeled)
- Cinnamon (1 tsp)
- Ginger (1 tsp powdered)

Green Smoothie with Orange and Ginger

This recipe can be ready in 5 minutes, makes 2 servings (48 oz.), and will take approximately 45 seconds of blending assuming you are using a blender that is 1000 watts.

Nutrition Information
300 calories
40 g of carbs
0 g of fat (saturated)
50 mg of sodium
2 g of fat
12 g of fiber
10 g of protein
28 g of sugar

Ingredients

- Spinach (2 c packed tightly)
- Water (1.5 c)
- Romain lettuce (1 c packed tightly)
- Banana (2 peeled)
- Navel orange (2 peeled)
- Cucumber (1 peeled and chopped)
- Ginger (1 inch)

Green Smoothie with Mint and Blueberries

This recipe can be ready in 5 minutes, makes 1 serving (24 oz.), and will take approximately 45 seconds of blending assuming you are using a blender that is 1000 watts.

Nutrition Information
230 calories
50 g of carbs
5 g of protein
11 g of fiber
35 g of sugar
200 mg of sodium
1.5 g of fat
0 g of fat (saturated)

Ingredients

- Blueberries (2 c)
- Spinach (2 c)
- Mint leaves (4 crushed)
- Kiwi (1 peeled)
- Coconut water (1 c)
- Ice (1 c)

Green Smoothie with Kale and Pineapple

This recipe can be ready in 5 minutes, makes 1 serving (24 oz.), and will take approximately 45 seconds of blending assuming you are using a blender that is 1000 watts.

Nutrition Information
350 calories
8 g of fat
19 g of sugar
12 g of fiber
6 g of protein
3 g of fat (saturated)
45 g of carbs

Ingredients

- Kale (1 c)
- Cucumber (1 c)
- Cilantro (1 c)
- Lemon Juice (1 tsp.)
- Avocado (.5 peeled)

Rolled Oats Breakfast Smoothie

This recipe can be ready in 5 minutes, makes 1 serving (24 oz.), and will take approximately 45 seconds of blending assuming you are using a blender that is 1000 watts.

Nutrition Information
260 calories
8 g of fat
16 g of sugar
40 g of carbs
11 g of protein
6 g of fiber
114 mg of sodium
3 g of fat (saturated)

Ingredients

- Milk (.75 c)
- Banana (1)
- Rolled oats (.25 cups uncooked)
- Spinach (2 c tightly packed)
- Flax seed (2 T)

Honeydew Smoothie with Lime

This recipe can be ready in 5 minutes, makes 4 servings (24 oz. each), and will take approximately 45 seconds of blending assuming you are using a blender that is 1000 watts.

Nutrition Information
240 calories
4 g of protein
15 g of carbs
50 mg of sodium
4 g of fat (saturated)
17 g of sugar
4 g of fiber
9 g of fat

Ingredients

- Honeydew (4 c)
- Mint leaves (1 c)
- Coconut milk (.5 c)
- Ice (1 c)
- Lime juice (1 tsp.)

Peaches and Kale Smoothie

This recipe can be ready in 5 minutes, makes 1 serving (24 oz.), and will take approximately 45 seconds of blending assuming you are using a blender that is 1000 watts.

Nutrition Information
400 calories
34 g of sugar
33 g of protein
2 g of fiber
600 mg of sodium
60 g of carbs
2.5 g of fat (saturated)
9 g of fat

Ingredients

- Frozen peaches (1 c)
- Protein powder (20 g)
- Almond milk (1 c)
- Banana (1 peeled)
- Pineapple (1 c frozen)
- Flaxseed (1 T)
- Kale (2 c)

Pineapple Avocado Smoothie

THIS RECIPE CAN BE READY IN 5 MINUTES, MAKES 2 SERVINGS (12 OZ. EACH), AND WILL TAKE APPROXIMATELY 45 SECONDS OF BLENDING ASSUMING YOU ARE USING A BLENDER THAT IS 1000 WATTS.

Nutrition Information
169 calories
20 g of carbs
6 g of fat
6 g of sugar
18 g of protein
4 g of fiber
0 g of fat (saturated)
345 mg of sodium

INGREDIENTS

- Kale (2 c packed tightly)
- Almond milk (.5 c)
- Pineapple (.5 c chunked)
- Protein powder (20 g)
- Avocado (.5 peeled)
- Ice cubes (1 c)

AGAVE, SPINACH AND KALE SMOOTHIE

This recipe can be ready in 5 minutes, makes 2 servings (24 oz. each), and will take approximately 45 seconds of blending assuming you are using a blender that is 1000 watts.

Nutrition Information
300 calories
80 mg of sodium
5 g of protein
40 g of carbs
8 g of fat (saturated)
9 g of fiber
16 g of sugar
15 g of fat

Ingredients

- Coconut milk (.5 c)
- Coconut water (1 c)
- Agave syrup (1 T)
- Pear (1 peeled, cored)
- Lime juice (1 lime)
- Spinach (2 c)
- Kale (2 c)

SPICY GREEN SMOOTHIE

THIS RECIPE CAN BE READY IN 5 MINUTES, MAKES 1 SERVING (24 OZ.), AND WILL TAKE APPROXIMATELY 45 SECONDS OF BLENDING ASSUMING YOU ARE USING A BLENDER THAT IS 1000 WATTS.

Nutrition Information
260 calories
32 g of carbs
14 g of sugar
4 g of fat (saturated)
12 g of fat
125 mg of sodium
8 g of protein
6 g of fiber

INGREDIENTS

- Cayenne pepper (1 tsp)
- Avocado (.5 peeled)
- Coconut water (1 c)
- Kale (1 c)
- Frozen pineapple (.5 c)
- Spinach (1 c)

Honey and Spinach Smoothie

This recipe can be ready in 5 minutes, makes 1 serving (24 oz.), and will take approximately 45 seconds of blending assuming you are using a blender that is 1000 watts.

Nutrition Information
300 calories
4 g of fat
1 g of fiber
45 g of protein
25 g of carbs
19 g of sugar
2 g of fat (saturated)
140 mg of sodium

Ingredients

- Honey (1 T)
- Spinach (1 c)
- Protein powder (20 grams)
- Ice (1 c)
- Ice water (5 oz)

Apple and Greens Smoothie

This recipe can be ready in 5 minutes, makes 1 serving (24 oz.), and will take approximately 45 seconds of blending assuming you are using a blender that is 1000 watts.

Nutrition Information
290 calories
600 mg of sodium
2 g of fat (saturated)
28 g of protein
34 g of carbs
23 g of sugar
7 g of fiber
6 g of fat

Ingredients

- Kale (1 c)
- Spinach (1 c)
- Almond milk (1 c)
- Cucumber (1 chopped)
- Protein powder (20 g)
- Green apple (1 cored)
- Lemon juice (1 tsp)

Avocado and Lime Smoothie

This recipe can be ready in 5 minutes, makes 1 serving (24 oz.), and will take approximately 45 seconds of blending assuming you are using a blender that is 1000 watts.

Nutrition Information
340 calories
10 g of protein
34 g of carbs
19 g of sugar
9 g of fiber
8 g of fat (saturated)
50 mg of sodium
22 g of fat

Ingredients

- Baby spinach (.5 c)
- Lime (1 peeled)
- Lime zest (1 lime)
- Almond milk (1 c)
- Avocado (.5 peeled)
- Vanilla extract (.5 tsp)
- Honey (.5 T)
- Vanilla extract (.5 tsp)

- Sea salt (1 tsp)

BASIL AND CHLORELLA SMOOTHIE

THIS RECIPE CAN BE READY IN 5 MINUTES, MAKES 1 SERVING (24 OZ.), AND WILL TAKE APPROXIMATELY 45 SECONDS OF BLENDING ASSUMING YOU ARE USING A BLENDER THAT IS 1000 WATTS.

Nutrition Information
320 calories
240 mg of sodium
15 g of fat
10 g of fiber
4 g of fat (saturated
13 g of protein
35 g of carbs
22 g of sugar

INGREDIENTS

- Frozen pineapple (.5 c chunks)
- Coconut water (1 c)
- Avocado (.5 peeled)
- Basil (6 leaves)
- Plain yoghurt (.25 c)
- Chia seeds (1 tsp)

- Maca (1 tsp)
- Chlorella (1 tsp)
- Lemon juice (1 tsp)
- Bee pollen (1 tsp)
- Sea salt (1 tsp)
- Honey (.5 T)

Berries and Beets Smoothie

This recipe can be ready in 5 minutes, makes 1 serving (24 oz.), and will take approximately 45 seconds of blending assuming you are using a blender that is 1000 watts.

Nutrition Information
280 calories
30 mg of sodium
7 g of fat (saturated)
21 g of sugar
4 g of protein
38 g of carbs
15 g of fiber
15 g of fat

Ingredients

- Coconut oil (1 T)
- Ginger (2 tsp)
- Beet greens (.5 c)
- Beets (.5 c cooked)
- Water (1 c)
- Frozen raspberries (.5 c)
- Lemon (1 peeled)
- Frozen blackberries (.5 c)

Dandelion Smoothie with Lime

This recipe can be ready in 5 minutes, makes 1 serving (24 oz.), and will take approximately 45 seconds of blending assuming you are using a blender that is 1000 watts.

Nutrition Information
190 calories
1 g of fat
43 g of carbs
80 mg of sodium
6 g of fiber
7 g of protein
0 g of fat (saturated)
25 g of sugar

Ingredients

- Lemon juice (1 peeled)
- Frozen banana (1 peeled)
- Water (1 c)
- Spirulina (.5 tsp)
- Dandelion greens (1.5 cups destemmed)
- Chlorella (1 tsp)
- Honey (.5 T)
- Ice cubes (7)

- Pink Himalayan salt (1 tsp)

Avocado and Mango Smoothie

This recipe can be ready in 5 minutes, makes 1 serving (24 oz.), and will take approximately 45 seconds of blending assuming you are using a blender that is 1000 watts.

Nutrition Information
314 calories
16 g of fat
5 g of protein
100 mg of sodium
48 g of carbs
30 g of sugar
3 g of fat (saturated)
11 g of fiber

Ingredients

- Avocado (1 peeled)
- Cilantro (.5 c)
- Water (1 c)
- Frozen mango (1 c)
- Line juice (1 lime)
- Spinach (1 c)

- Ginger (.25 inch)
- Raw honey (.5 T)

GUACAMOLE SMOOTHIE

THIS RECIPE CAN BE READY IN 5 MINUTES, MAKES 1 SERVING (24 OZ.), AND WILL TAKE APPROXIMATELY 45 SECONDS OF BLENDING ASSUMING YOU ARE USING A BLENDER THAT IS 1000 WATTS.

Nutrition Information
350 calories
7 g of fat (saturated)
30 g of fat
250 mg of sodium
24 g of carbs
4 g of sugar
15 g of fiber
5 g of protein

INGREDIENTS

- Avocado (1 peeled)
- Tomato (1 c)
- Water (1 c)
- Line juice (.25 c)
- Sea salt (1 tsp)

- Cilantro (.5 c)

Spinach and Strawberry Smoothie

This recipe can be ready in 5 minutes, makes 1 serving (24 oz.), and will take approximately 45 seconds of blending assuming you are using a blender that is 1000 watts.

Nutrition Information
500 calories
200 mg of sodium
8 g of fat (saturated)
15 g of fat
32 g of sugar
45 g of carbs
12 g of protein
13 g of fiber

Ingredients

- Banana (1 peeled)
- Spinach (1 c)
- Almond milk (1.5 c)
- Frozen strawberries (.5 c)
- Plain Greek yogurt (2)
- Frozen mango (.5 c)
- Chia seeds (1 T)
- Bee pollen (1 tsp)

- Coconut oil (1 T)

Immune system boosting smoothies

Cinnamon and Spinach Smoothie

This recipe can be ready in 5 minutes, makes 1 serving (24 oz.), and will take approximately 45 seconds of blending assuming you are using a blender that is 1000 watts.

Nutrition Information
304 calories
105 mg of sodium
15 g of fat
3 g of protein
46 g of carbs
7 g of fiber
20 g of sugar
3 g of fat (saturated)

Ingredients

- Frozen banana (1 peeled)
- Spinach (1 c)
- Water (1 c)
- Frozen blackberries (1 c)
- Basil (5 leaves)
- Cinnamon (.25 tsp)
- Coconut oil (1 T)
- Stevia (1 tsp)

Wheatgrass and Goji Berry Smoothie

This recipe can be ready in 5 minutes, makes 1 serving (24 oz.), and will take approximately 45 seconds of blending assuming you are using a blender that is 1000 watts.

Nutrition Information
500 calories
22 g of fat
15 g of protein
200 mg of sodium
50 g of carbs
29 g of sugar
20 g of fiber
1 gram of fat (saturated)

Ingredients

- Wheatgrass (1 tsp powdered)
- Stevia (1 tsp)
- Coconut oil (1 T)
- Coconut flakes (1 T)
- Maca (1 tsp)
- Dried cranberries (2 T)
- Greek yoghurt (.5 c)
- Goji berries (2 T)

- Kale (.5 c)
- Frozen mango (.5 c)
- Spinach (.5 c)
- Coconut water (1 c)
- Avocado (.5 peeled)

Aloe Vera and Blueberry Smoothie

This recipe can be ready in 5 minutes, makes 1 serving (24 oz.), and will take approximately 45 seconds of blending assuming you are using a blender that is 1000 watts.

Nutrition Information
275 calories
3 g of fat (saturated)
30 g of carbs
7 g of fiber
45 mg of sodium
17 g of fat
3 g of protein
24 g of sugar

Ingredients

- Aloe vera (.5 cups)
- Avocado (.5 peeled)
- Water (1 c)
- Frozen blueberries (.5 c)
- Coconut oil (.5 T)
- Spinach (1 c)
- Pink Himalayan salt (1 T)
- Stevia (.5 tsp)

- Coconut oil (.5 T)

STRAWBERRY SMOOTHIE WITH MINT

THIS RECIPE CAN BE READY IN 5 MINUTES, MAKES 1 SERVING (24 OZ.), AND WILL TAKE APPROXIMATELY 45 SECONDS OF BLENDING ASSUMING YOU ARE USING A BLENDER THAT IS 1000 WATTS.

Nutrition Information
160 calories
20 g of sugar
40 g of carbs
0 g of fat (saturated)
12 g of fiber
3 g of protein
300 mg of sodium
1 g of fat

INGREDIENTS

- Frozen banana (1 peeled)
- Frozen strawberries (1 c)
- Water (1 c)
- Mint leaves (2 c)
- Spinach (1 c)
- Stevia (1 tsp)

Banana and Rosemary Smoothie

This recipe can be ready in 5 minutes, makes 1 serving (24 oz.), and will take approximately 45 seconds of blending assuming you are using a blender that is 1000 watts.

Nutrition Information
200 calories
50 g of carbs
232 mg of sodium
1 gram of fat
29 g of sugar
9 g of fiber
3 g of protein
0 g of fat (saturated)

Ingredients

- Frozen banana (1 peeled)
- Blueberries (1 c)
- Water (1 c)
- Rosemary (2 sprigs)
- Sea salt (1 tsp)
- Stevia (1 tsp)

BEET GREENS AND CINNAMON SMOOTHIE

THIS RECIPE CAN BE READY IN 5 MINUTES, MAKES 1 SERVING (24 OZ.), AND WILL TAKE APPROXIMATELY 45 SECONDS OF BLENDING ASSUMING YOU ARE USING A BLENDER THAT IS 1000 WATTS.

Nutrition Information
200 calories
1 gram of fat
10 g of fiber
75 mg of sodium
25 g of sugar
0 g of fat (saturated)
50 g of carbs
3 g of protein

INGREDIENTS

- Green apple (1 cored)
- Frozen blueberries (.5 c)
- Water (1 c)
- Frozen banana (1 peeled)
- Cinnamon (1 tsp)
- Beet greens (1.5 c)
- Stevia (1 tsp)

Spinach and Mint Smoothie

This recipe can be ready in 5 minutes, makes 1 serving (24 oz.), and will take approximately 45 seconds of blending assuming you are using a blender that is 1000 watts.

Nutrition Information
230 calories
3 g of fat (saturated)
7 g of fiber
75 mg of sodium
23 g of sugar
40 g of carbs
4 g of protein
8 g of fat

Ingredients

- Frozen banana (1 peeled)
- Spinach (1 c)
- Almond milk (1 c)
- Frozen blueberries (1 c)
- Coconut oil (1 T)
- Mint leaves (1 cup)
- Stevia (1 tsp)

Kale Smoothie with Blueberries

This recipe can be ready in 5 minutes, makes 1 serving (24 oz.), and will take approximately 45 seconds of blending assuming you are using a blender that is 1000 watts.

Nutrition Information
367 calories
13 g of fat
75 mg of sodium
25 g of sugar
50 g of carbs
10 g of fiber
20 g of protein
6 g of fat (saturated)

Ingredients

- Frozen blueberries (.5 c)
- Almond milk (1 c)
- Frozen banana (1 peeled)
- Cinnamon (.5 tsp)
- Kale (1 c)
- Stevia (1 tsp)
- Coconut oil (1 T)

Banana and Beets Smoothie

This recipe can be ready in 5 minutes, makes 1 serving (24 oz.), and will take approximately 45 seconds of blending assuming you are using a blender that is 1000 watts.

Nutrition Information
150 calories
3 g of fat
10 g of fiber
25 g of sugar
75 mg of sodium
0 g of fat (saturated)
50 g of carbs
3 g of protein

Ingredients

- Beet greens (1 c chopped)
- Frozen banana (1 peeled)
- Chia seeds (1 T)
- Water (1 c)
- Coconut oil (1 T)
- Stevia (1 tsp)

Mixed Berry and Lettuce Smoothie

This recipe can be ready in 5 minutes, makes 1 serving (24 oz.), and will take approximately 45 seconds of blending assuming you are using a blender that is 1000 watts.

Nutrition Information
190 calories
0 g of fat (saturated)
45 g of carbs
8 g of fiber
25 g of sugar
210 mg of sodium
4 g of protein
1 gram of fat

Ingredients

- Red apple (1 cored)
- Cinnamon (.25 tsp)
- Kale (1 cup)
- Water (1 cup)
- Pink Himalayan salt (1 tsp)
- Frozen banana (1 peeled)
- Stevia (1 tsp)

GREENS ON GREENS SMOOTHIE

THIS RECIPE CAN BE READY IN 5 MINUTES, MAKES 1 SERVING (24 OZ.), AND WILL TAKE APPROXIMATELY 45 SECONDS OF BLENDING ASSUMING YOU ARE USING A BLENDER THAT IS 1000 WATTS.

Nutrition Information
140 calories
15 g of sugar
2 g of fat
4 g of protein
35 g of carbs
150 mg of sodium
4 g of fiber
0 g of fat (saturated)

INGREDIENTS

- Kale (1 c)
- Baby spinach (1 c)
- Coconut flakes (.25 cups)
- Frozen banana (1 peeled)
- Water (1 c)
- Coconut oil (1 T)

Apples, Apples, Apples Green Smoothie

This recipe can be ready in 5 minutes, makes 1 serving (24 oz.), and will take approximately 45 seconds of blending assuming you are using a blender that is 1000 watts.

Nutrition Information
300 calories
32 g of sugar
9 g of fiber
1 gram of fat (saturated)
300 mg of sodium
60 g of carbs
3 g of protein
5 g of fat

Ingredients

- Red apple (1 cored)
- Green apple (1 cored)
- Yellow apple (1 cored)
- Coconut oil (1 T)
- Baby spinach (1 c)
- Cinnamon (.5 tsp)
- Water (1 c)
- Maca (.5 T)

Banana and Mint Smoothie

This recipe can be ready in 5 minutes, makes 1 serving (24 oz.), and will take approximately 45 seconds of blending assuming you are using a blender that is 1000 watts.

Nutrition Information
280 calories
25 g of sugar
6 g of fiber
0 g of fat (saturated)
75 mg of sodium
35 g of carbs
10 g of protein
12 g of fat

Ingredients

- Frozen blueberries (1 c)
- Chia seeds (1 T)
- Almond milk (1 c)
- Mint leaves (10)
- Frozen banana (1 peeled)
- Water (1 c)
- Stevia (1 tsp)
- Coconut oil (1 T)

Strawberry and Salad Smoothie

This recipe can be ready in 5 minutes, makes 1 serving (24 oz.), and will take approximately 45 seconds of blending assuming you are using a blender that is 1000 watts.

Nutrition Information
200 calories
125 mg of sodium
6 g of fat
7 g of fiber
20 g of sugar
40 g of carbs
0 g of fat (saturated)
3 g of protein

Ingredients

- Frozen strawberries (1 c)
- Sea salt (1 tsp)
- Flax seed (1 T)
- Salad greens (1 c)
- Water (1 c)
- Kale (.5 c)
- Cinnamon (1 tsp)
- Frozen banana (1 peeled)

- Stevia (1 tsp)
- Coconut oil (1 T)

Conclusion

Smoothies are designed to replace a regular meal and because they have fewer calories and help suppress appetite until the following meal you don't feel hungry. As part of your diet you need to ensure that you are consuming the right amount of vitamins and nutrients most of which you can get from drinking a smoothie each day.

Smoothies should not be used to replace your entire nutrition source rather they should be used in addition to a healthy diet and exercise routine. If you can then you should make your own smoothies at home, this allows you to control the ingredients and minimize any unnecessary calories.

If you're completely new to smoothies, it is well worth your time search your cook books for a tried and tested smoothie recipe to start with and altering it to your taste as necessary. Most smoothies are seen as good ways to lose weight, as long as you avoid the ones loaded with chocolate or ice cream.

There is nothing magical about losing weight, you achieve it through consuming less calories and research has found that people who consumed fruit smoothies have been able to lose up to 3 times more weight than those who consumed ate regular food.

However, this decrease in calories can only happen if you replace one of your meals or large snacks with a smoothie.

One great ingredient to use in almost any smoothie is bananas, the texture of the banana makes the smoothie resemble a milk shake.

The best way to use bananas in a smoothie is to let the bananas get to the point where they are lightly spotted, and then peel them and put them in freezer bag. The banana in a weight loss smoothie provides energy and if you add milk and yogurt they will provide calcium and protein.

If you use the right ingredients in your smoothie you can boost your energy and your metabolism as well as at the same time you are getting the essential vitamins and minerals that you need and curbing your appetite.

If your smoothie is high in protein then it can help keep your metabolism high, which in turn can give you a boost of energy that can take you all the way to your next meal without the urge to snack. The higher your metabolism then the better the body processes fat into energy.

www.ingramcontent.com/pod-product-compliance
Lightning Source LLC
Chambersburg PA
CBHW071441070526
44578CB00001B/175